Horizons of Shamanism

A Triangular Approach to the History and Anthropology of Ecstatic Techniques

Marjorie Mandelstam Balzer, Jan N. Bremmer and Carlo Ginzburg

Edited by Peter Jackson

STOCKHOLM
UNIVERSITY PRESS

Published by
Stockholm University Press
Stockholm University
SE-106 91 Stockholm, Sweden
www.stockholmuniversitypress.se

First published 2016
Cover Illustration: © Creative Commons Zero (CC0)
Cover designed by Karl Edqvist, SUP

Stockholm Studies in Comparative Religion (Online) ISSN: 0562-1070

ISBN (Paperback): 978-91-7635-027-0
ISBN (PDF): 978-91-7635-024-9
ISBN (EPUB): 978-91-7635-025-6
ISBN (Kindle): 978-91-7635-026-3

DOI: http://dx.doi.org/10.16993/bag

Suggested citation:
Jackson, P. (ed.) 2016 *Horizons of Shamanism: A Triangular Approach to
the History and Anthropology of Ecstatic Techniques*. Stockholm: Stockholm
University Press. DOI: http://dx.doi.org/10.16993/bag

To read the free, open access version of this book online,
visit http://dx.doi.org/10.16993/bag or scan this QR code
with your mobile device.

Stockholm Studies in Comparative Religion

Stockholm Studies in Comparative Religion (SSCR) is a peer-reviewed series initiated by Åke Hultkrantz in 1961.

While its earlier emphasis lay in ethnographic-comparative approaches to religion, the series now covers a broader spectrum of the history of religions, including the philological study of discrete traditions, large-scale comparisons between different traditions as well as theoretical and methodological concerns in the study of cross-cultural religious categories such as ritual and myth.

SSCR strives to sustain and disseminate high-quality and innovative research in the form of monographs and edited volumes, preferably in English, but in exceptional cases also in French, German, and Scandinavian languages.

SSCR was previously included in the series Acta Universitatis Stockholmiensis (ISSN 0562-1070). A full list of publications can be found here: http://doi.org/10.16993/sup.s1

Editorial board

Olof Sundqvist, Professor, Department for Ethnology, History of Religions and Gender Studies at Stockholm University.

Titles in the series

36. Jackson, P. (ed.) 2016. *Horizons of Shamanism. A Triangular Approach to the History and Anthropology of Ecstatic Techniques.* Stockholm: Stockholm University Press. License: CC-BY 4.0

Contents

Preface

Peter Jackson
Stockholm University, Sweden

The substance of this book grows out of a workshop on shamans and shamanism held in the Fall of 2013 to mark the 100th anniversary of the chair in History of Religions at Stockholm University. In considering an adequate theme for the workshop, we decided on the idea of engaging various theoretical and empirical approaches to a singular cultural matrix. We were also anxious to pick a theme that could be considered representative of the work of the department's most prolific scholars over the decades. The theme of shamanism eventually stood out as the most appropriate choice – not only because it recurs extensively in the department's publications, but also because shamanism has become such a multifarious category in contemporary scholarship. Like most other categories of its kind, it has been contested, reinterpreted, and engrafted into various jargons both within and outside the academic world.

As representatives of disciplines bordering on the history of religions, the three main contributors to the workshop (and to the ensuing publication) embody the spirit of comparativism and multidisciplinarity without which the study of religion always runs the risk of relapsing into a sacred science (or a science of the sacred). They are all internationally acknowledged interlocutors within their fields of expertise: Marjorie Mandelstam Balzer (Georgetown University) is a leading expert on contemporary Siberian shamanism, Jan Bremmer (University of Groningen) a prominent specialist on ancient Graeco-Roman religions, and Carlo Ginzburg (UCLA and the Scuola Normale Superiore di Pisa) one of the world's most renowned historians.

How to cite this book chapter:
Jackson, P. 2016. Preface. In: Jackson, P. (ed.) *Horizons of Shamanism: A Triangular Approach to the History and Anthropology of Ecstatic Techniques*. Pp. vi–x. Stockholm: Stockholm University Press. DOI: http:// dx.doi.org/10.16993/bag.a. License: CC-BY 4.0

Balzer's contribution intertwines a series of hitherto ignored topics with regard to the formerly repressed shamans of post-Soviet Russia, Bremmer brings further light to the controversial status of "shamanism" in the study of ancient Greek religion, and Ginzburg revisits a theme first developed in his study from 1972 on the surprisingly shamanic traits of the so-called *benandanti* (the "well-goers"), a group of alleged heretics described in a 16th-century inquisition file from Friuli in northern Italy. In the introduction and afterword, associate professor Ulf Drobin (Stockholm University) discusses the three contributions against the backdrop of earlier and more recent trends in the study of shamanism. Drobin also engages in a critical dialogue with Bremmer and Ginzburg on the origin and geographical distribution of shamanistic techniques.

When the chair for the History of Religions was established in Stockholm in 1913 it was explicitly done in a spirit of secularism. The much older universities of Uppsala and Lund had offered theological teaching for centuries, but theology there usually meant the study of a specific religious tradition – its sacred history, canon, and institutions – *by, for,* and *from within itself*: its closest ally had been the Church and its major body of students consisted of future clergy. However, religiously informed scholarship was rapidly losing ground in 19th-century Europe. The gradual diminution of theology and religious teaching in the academic world corresponded inversely to an increasing sense of time depth and cultural complexity, fuelled by the study of ancient languages and civilizations, ethnography, geology, and evolutionary biology. A new story of humankind was unfolding, much more layered and detailed than the Biblical and antiquarian narratives of previous centuries. Of course, systematic comparative studies of religion had been pursued much earlier, but it was only during the latter half of the 19th-century that the secular study of religion emerged as a university discipline in its own right.

The establishment of the Stockholm chair clearly reflected this new university policy. The same trend had recently resulted in the creation of similar academic units elsewhere in Europe. The most significant measure in this regard was perhaps the creation, 27 years earlier, in 1886, of a new section for the religious sciences at the École Pratique des Hautes Études (EPHE) in Paris. Along with the donation for the Stockholm chair came the donators' explicit wish to establish the study of religion as a contingent cultural phenomenon, whose change and diversity in time and space should be subjected to methodological ideals attuned to those of comparative linguistics and archaeology.

The first holder of the chair, Torgny Segerstedt, was a controversial figure in his time, provoking Swedish old-school theologians with his Uppsala dissertation on the origin of polytheism. Having left the Stockholm chair in 1917 to embark on a new career as a publicist, Segerstedt spent the last years of his life, between 1933 and 1945, attacking a new and much fiercer enemy to freedom of thought and critical scholarship than the Swedish conservative theologians of his early days: German Nazism.

If the secular study of religion had first emerged as an emancipation from the scholarly dictate of religion itself, an important step was taken during the latter half of the 20th-century to overcome the discipline's methodological restrictions. Historians of religions had not been expected to conduct their own field-work, but to stay at home with their texts and grammars, occasionally glancing through ethnographic reports. When the fourth holder of the chair in Stockholm, Åke Hultkrantz, began his field-work among the Shoshone people in Wyoming in the late 1940s, he was a pioneer in bringing the study of religion further beyond the religious heritage of its own past. The empirical framework of the history of religions was no longer restricted to the authority of scripture, but had widened its scope to include participant observation, and to the gathering of new data in the midst of action and conversation.

When I consider the research currently being carried out at the department, I gladly acknowledge a continued emphasis on both field-work and philological training. The impact from the social sciences on the study of religion has increased rapidly during the last decades. This is all fine and well, but if the confidence in this new asset grows too strong, it may give in to a trivialization and relativization of historical knowledge and serious philological research – a tendency felt in many areas of the humanities today. The past amounts to more than its modern reception and construction, to more than an imaginary past imbued with patriotic, romantic, and orientalist infatuations. Philology is certainly not only a mossy thing *of the past*; on the contrary, it increases the student's theoretical alertness and incites critical reconsideration, not so much through the emulation of ingrained theoretical postures but through careful first-hand reading.

As historians of religions we are blessed and cursed by the fact that religion pops up everywhere. Cursed because a growing sense of detail may discourage the increasingly specialized scholar to search for general patterns. Blessed because we are still entitled to combine comparative analysis with the interrogation, development, and rectification of analytical categories (such as myth, ritual, the sacred, and so on) that may ensue from, and feed back into, the understanding of a specific historical datum. This circumstance brings me back to the topic of this volume, for the shaman, and the accompanying *-ism* added to this once local and emic concept, is precisely one of those analytical categories that historians of religions have grappled with in order to discover general patterns beyond the locally specific manifestations of singular cultures.[1] Traceable back to Ernst Arbman's work on ecstatic practices and conceptions of the soul, the theme runs neatly through the rich production of Åke Hultkrantz, Louise Bäckman, and the last holder of the Stockholm chair, Per-Arne Berglie.

It has been a stimulating task to plan the event that now finally comes into fruition in the form of a physical publication. This would not have happened without the moral and financial support of vice chancellors Kåre Bremer and Astrid Söderbergh Widding, for which I – also speaking on the behalf of my colleagues – remain deeply grateful. I also wish to thank Christina Lenz at Stockholm University Press for her patience and efficacy during the final stages of editing the book. Many thanks also go to Klas Wikström af Edholm for doing a great job in copyediting the manuscript as well as preparing an index.

Notes

1. As demonstrated by Arnold van Gennep's 1903 paper "De l'emploi du mot 'chamanisme'" in *Revue de l'histoire des religions* (42:1), the

critique of the analytical category "shamanism" has a history nearly as long as the initial propagation of the category by the Russian scholar V. M. Mikhailovsky in the late 19th-century. In van Gennep's view, Western scholars of religion had merely created confusion for themselves by inventing such concepts, including those of animism and totemism. The critique has been rehearsed on several occasions and from shifting angles, a recent example being Håkan Rydving's 2011 essay *Le chamanisme aujourd'hui: Constructions et déconstructions d'une illusion scientifique* in *Études mongoles et Sibériennes, centrasiatiques et tibétaine* (42), which received a critical response from Charles Stépanoff in the following issue of the same journal. Problems related to the construction of this occidental category are also touched upon in the 2015 overview monograph *Le chamanisme* by Roberte Hamayon. Åke Hultkrantz, while stressing the import of the term "shamanism", insisted that it denoted a specific configuration of religious elements and not necessarily a religion (see, for instance, the article "A Definition of Shamanism" [Temenos 9 {1973}]).

Introduction

Ulf Drobin
Stockholm University, Sweden

Torgny Segerstedt is the most publicly well known representative that the Department of Comparative Religion has ever had, and it is thanks to him that it was possible to initiate such a department in Stockholm. He, if anyone, was a man of polemics. During the war, as a newspaperman, editor-in-chief of *Göteborgs Handels- och Sjöfarts-Tidning*, he was the clearest anti-Nazi voice in the country. But he was also a source of considerable anxiety to the war-time coalition government, whose prime concern it was to keep the country balancing on the difficult and dangerous tightrope of neutrality in order to avoid a German occupation. As professor of the history of religions he was – outside the theological faculty – more conventional and less dedicated: he resigned from the professorship after only three years.[1]

The two persons that meant the most for the Stockholm department's development and distinctive character are Professors Ernst Arbman and Åke Hultkrantz. The distinctiveness lay in the anthropological-folkloristic perspective they gave to the department; the choice of subjects in particular was the concept(s) of the soul and shamanism.

Arbman (1891–1959) graduated in theology at the University of Uppsala in 1914. He continued his studies there, majoring in Sanskrit, and in 1922 completed his doctoral thesis "Rudra. Untersuchungen zum altindischen Glauben und Kultus",[2] a religio-historical work within the framework of Indology. The dissertation made him docent/ associate professor in Indian philology and in the following year also in the history of religions. In 1933 Arbman became head of the department and acting professor of the history of religions at Stockholm's Högskola (as Stockholm University was called then). In

How to cite this book chapter:
Drobin, U. 2016. Introduction. In: Jackson, P. (ed.) *Horizons of Shamanism: A Triangular Approach to the History and Anthropology of Ecstatic Techniques*. Pp. xi–xx. Stockholm: Stockholm University Press. DOI: http://dx.doi.org/10.16993/bag.b. License: CC-BY 4.0

1937 he was called to the professorial chair of history of religions, a position that he kept until his retirement in 1958. Arbman died suddenly and unexpectedly during the year after his retirement.

Ernst Arbman had wide interests within the history of religions. One such interest was in the meaning of the concept of "soul". Buddha denied the existence of a soul but nevertheless believed in *samsara*, loosely translated as "transmigration of souls": what was it then that transmigrated? Here, Arbman tried to find more original Indian conceptions that should have preceded the advanced philosophical terms found in Buddhism.[3] At the same time, he was of course also interested in the concept of the soul because it was the point of departure for the evolutionistic theory proposed by Edward Tylor, a theory that was much discussed at that time. As a consequence Arbman developed a strong interest in the conceptions and worldviews of non-literate peoples. This would be called comparative anthropology in today's language, and he, in his own geographical sphere, extended this interest to Saami and the Old Norse religions. In addition to this he had a deep interest in the psychology of religion. The concept of the soul was to him primarily a psychological concept.

His magnum opus is *Ecstasy or Religious Trance. In the Experience of the Ecstatics and from the Psychological Point of View*. It consists of three parts: 1) Vision and Ecstasy; 2) Essence and Forms of Ecstasy; and 3) Ecstasy and Psychopathological States.[4] Examples referred to come from many areas of religion, not least from Catholic mystics. The tomes comprise 1705 pages. This was the result of more than two decades of research and his manuscripts were at the time of his death in 1959 in an unorganized and incomplete state.

The starting point for this huge work came from reflections concerning the Old Norse shamanism, or *seiðr* in Old Norse language. After Arbman's death, Åke Hultkrantz, his pupil and successor, completed the arduous task of editing *Ecstasy* with the aid of a colleague.

In my opinion *Ecstasy or Religious Trance* is a gold mine for the research on psychology of religion and for anyone interested in this subject. Unfortunately this great work has not received the attention and distribution it deserves. Stylistically Arbman wrote in a somewhat old fashioned, hypotactic Swedish modelled on the Latin periodic syntax. Originally, he both wrote in and had his works translated into German as well. The German language can support such hypotactic syntax better than Swedish; the opposite is true of English. In the 1930s he chose to publish in English for ideological reasons. Due to lack of both time and funds – and without Arbman's assistance – his translator was unable to render the Swedish text of *Ecstasy* into syntactically normal English but transcribed the Swedish virtually word for word into an English that causes an alienating impression on the reader. If one overcomes the surprise that the texts are written in an "artificial" language and simply reads, one discovers that they are fully logical and comprehensible and extraordinarily interesting! The three parts were published in English in 1963, 1968 and 1970 by the Swedish publisher Norstedts in its Scandinavian University Books series.

Inspired by Arbman's interest in non-literate peoples' conceptions of the soul as well as of the practice of shamanism, Åke Hultkrantz (1920–2006), besides studying the history of religions, acquired a solid education in ethnography (as anthropology was then named). Specializing in the study of North American Indians, he became licentiate in the history of religions *and* in ethnography in 1946. With its 545 pages, his doctoral thesis, *Conceptions of the Soul among North American Indians*,[5] which was submitted in 1953, is one of the largest dissertations ever presented at the faculty of humanities in Stockholm. This important dissertation earned him the position of docent/associate professor in the history of religions *and* docent competence in ethnography.[6]

In 1958, five years after Hultkrantz' dissertation, another doctoral thesis was published in Stockholm: *Die primitive Seelenvorstellungen der nordeurasischen Völker*, written by Ivar Paulson (1922–1966) – an Estonian war refugee in Sweden who, due to his background, was fluent in both Finnish and Russian.[7] The thesis gave Paulson the position of docent/associate professor in the history of religions. During these years, more might have been written on the concepts of the soul at our department than anywhere else in the world.

In 1961 Ivar Paulson published the monograph *Schutzgeister und Gottheiten des Wildes (der Jagdtiere und Fische) in Nordeurasien*.

Eine religionsetnographische und religionsphänomenologische Untersuchung jägerischer Glaubensvorstellungen.[8] This work has become a classic in the ethnographical literature on religion.

In 1962 Ivar Paulson, together with Åke Hultkrantz and the West German ethnographer Karl Jettmar, published *Die Religionen Nordeurasiens.* This book is the third volume of the large international series of books on the religions of the world entitled Die Religionen der Menschheit – which today consists of 33 volumes. This emphasizes how well established Hultkrantz and Paulson were in the field of international research on religion. In this volume Ivar Paulson wrote about the religions of the peoples of Siberia and of Finnish peoples and Hultkrantz about Saami religion, while Jettmar dealt with the archaeological evidence of North Eurasia's history of religions. Paulson died in 1966, only 44 years old.

Åke Hultkrantz was made full professor in 1958 at the age of 38. Through his ethnographic–anthropological schooling he came to have an innovative influence in the subject of history of religions. He gave visibility to non-literate peoples in the field of the subject, whereas earlier the Near East and India had dominated. Through his extensive reading of ethnographical, ethnological and folkloristic literature his knowledge was outstanding, especially concerning the formations of theories within those disciplines. This contributed to the expansion of the boundaries of the history of religions and to the refinement of the general cultural perspective of the discipline.

Åke Hultkrantz was a dedicated man. To him the history of religions was a vocation rather than a profession. He was always working: reading, lecturing and writing. His exceptionally good memory and stylistic gift allowed him to work faster than most of his colleagues. His bibliography is proof of this: it contains more than 25 monographs and when articles on scientific subjects are added it comprises 471 publications! Practically all of these publications were of the highest quality. The bibliography, compiled by Hultkrantz' wife, Geraldine Hultkrantz, is available through the department's home page to all who are interested. Åke Hultkrantz is known as one of the leading experts on North American Indians. Today he is far better known in the USA and

Canada than in Sweden. His international fame led researchers from these and other countries to come to our department to study and in some cases to take their Ph.D. on the religions of the North American Indians and in one case of the Inuit. Hultkrantz retired in 1986 and died in 2006 at the age of 86.

To conclude the history of the department of history of religions I maintain that it has sustained much of the distinctiveness and vitality that it had under the now deceased Arbman, Hultkrantz, Paulson, and others who are not mentioned here.

Among the living representatives for our subject the following successors to the chair should be mentioned: professors Louise Bäckman and Per-Arne Berglie. Louise Bäckman, herself a Saami, was attracted by Hultkrantz' intimate knowledge of the Saami culture and religion and by his ability to see the Saami in a wider geographical cultural context. She is a very valuable asset because of her inside perspective and her knowledge of the Saami language, i.e. having Saami as her mother tongue. The fact that she is a Saami also provided her access, as a researcher, to especially good contacts among the Saami. She and Hultkrantz have together written a monograph on Saami shamanism, *Studies in Lapp Shamanism*.[9]

Per-Arne Berglie's doctoral thesis is entitled *The Gods Descend. Ritual possession among the Sherpas and Tibetans*.[10] In his later research he has studied the beliefs and practices of spirit-mediums, primarily in Burma, an interest in line with that of Arbman's and Hultkrantz'.

As might be clear from this retrospect of the research history of the Stockholm department of history of religions, concepts of the soul and of shamanism have been at the forefront of the research and have also internationally become associated with our department.[11] I shall here describe, in a somewhat simplified form, the concepts of the soul that Arbman, Hultkrantz and Paulson, in the language of the time, called "primitive" concepts, by which they meant that the concepts were more original ones independent of Christian or other religious dogmatics. Arbman, Hultkrantz and Paulson designate the system of concepts of the soul, which they found globally (i.e. in ancient times in India, among North American Indians and among North Eurasian peoples), as "dualistic pluralism". They maintained that influential researchers such as Herbert Spencer and Edward Tylor had erroneously applied a uniform coherent (monistic) concept of the soul, which had become generally accepted.

Dualistic pluralism consists of the oppositional character between the so-called "body-souls", which are active when a person is awake, and the homogenous "free-soul", which represents the human being outside the body during dreams and shamanistic ecstasy.

Body-souls in turn consist of two spheres of concepts. On the one hand are "life-souls", which manifest the difference between life and death. To these phenomena belong breathing (breath-soul), the heart (heart-soul, etc.), the pulse, body heat, the gaze (the difference between the gaze of the living and the so-called broken gaze of the dead) and the blood. The life-soul is not to be seen as identical with its physical corporal basis. It expresses itself via the organ's function and the organ is the abode of the life-soul.

The second conceptual sphere is made up of the so-called "ego-souls", i.e. those which are the origins and bearers of man's psychic manifestations such as thought, memory, willpower and emotional life. Unlike the free-soul, these ego-souls are not expressions of the individual's whole personality, but represent different hypostasized psychic qualities such as love, empathy, courage, hate, jealousy etc., which are localized in different bodily organs such as the heart, liver, lungs, kidneys or gall bladder. These psychic properties are concretized to ego-souls and relate to bodily organs in the same way as the life-souls described above. The heart has a special position as a psychic organ. Expressions such as "broken heart" and even German's "Sinn" and English's "mind" might linguistically be derived from denotations of such ego-souls. Regarding the brain as the centre of thought and reasoning is of a much later date.[12]

The dead in the realm of the dead are often designated as "surviving-souls". It would be precipitate to believe that it is the free-soul that survives in the realm of the dead. The free-soul is thought of as the *living* person's manifestation beyond the body. Concepts of the dead in the realm of the dead are usually vaguer, and are often equated with the survivors' memorial picture of the deceased.

As Bremmer suggests, no research has been carried out to explain how the idea of the unitary soul arose. I think a possible guess could be to assume that when the "high religions" became, or were about to become, part of the state, the doctrine of punishment and bliss in the afterlife was developed, since the religion's function to socialize came into focus in a new way, and created a doctrine which, logically and morally, demanded complete identification between man in this life and in the afterlife.[13]

It should here already be emphasized that the concepts of the soul and of shamanism are related notions in the sense that the concept of the free-soul is a precondition for shamanism. In the dream the free-soul is believed to leave the body and to have experiences far beyond its owner's corporal limits. In shamanism, the shaman, using willpower, sends out his free-soul on expeditions to geographically distant places, or to other worlds, as the celestial world or the realm of the dead in the underworld. This possibility of the free-soul to act outside the body applies not only to the shaman's own free-soul, but also to those of others, as shown by phenomena such as the curing of "soul-loss" (where the shaman cures through finding the patient's disappeared free-soul, which perhaps has been captured by supernatural beings), or the shaman's acting as a "psychopomp" (when he aids the dead by taking the deceased's free-soul to the realm of the dead). And of course mediumism also occurs, at times unwillingly, but mostly willingly by possession by spirits as alternative or complimentary phenomena of acquiring supernatural knowledge. (In this case, the shaman has contact with the spirit world and has obtained a number of helping spirits, among other things.) However, the crucial criterion for shamanism still is the shaman's own free-soul journey.

* * *

When the department of history of religions decided to invite three prominent researchers as guest speakers, it was natural to choose shamanism as the theme. Carlo Ginzburg is a versatile and eminent historian, who through his book *Benandanti. The Night Battles* has cast a radically new light on both the Inquisition's early witch-trials and a hitherto unknown form of shamanism. He has written a detailed commentary on the Benandanti (339 pp.) in *Ecstasies. Deciphering the Witches' Sabbath*.[14]

To this could be added that according to Ginzburg it was Arne Runeberg's doctoral thesis, *Witches, Demons and Fertility Magic*,[15] that made Ginzburg aware of the connection between the concepts of witches and fertility cults. Runeberg was visiting associate professor (gästdocent) at the department of history of religions from 1962 to 1964 and a close friend of Åke Hultkrantz'. It can thus be maintained that for a long time there have been bonds between our department and Carlo Ginzburg, and a survey of his scientific production also bears witness to a considerable commonality of interests.

Jan Bremmer, who also has ties to our department, is a most knowledgeable historian of antiquity focussing on classical Greece. In 1983, Princeton University Press published *The Early Greek Concept of the Soul*,[16] where he follows the "dualistic pluralism" developed in Stockholm in his view of the phenomenology of the concepts of the soul. Bremmer's study of early Greek concepts of the soul has contributed to make the Stockholm investigations on the soul internationally known.

Marjorie Mandelstam Balzer is a well known and prestigious field researcher specializing, *inter alia*, on Siberian shamanism. She has been chosen as a guest speaker to guarantee that our discussions on shamans should not be about shamans merely as theoretical products but also as human beings of flesh and blood: the institute's first field researcher was Åke Hultkrantz – after him field research has almost been as natural for us as it is for a department of social anthropology.[17]

Notes

1. Ancker 1962; Hedin 2013.

2. Arbman 1922.

3. Arbman 1926–1927.

4. Arbman 1963; 1968; 1970.

5. Hultkrantz 1953.

6. It can be mentioned here that the thesis was re-published 44 years later, in 1997, this time in the USA, on an American initiative and in

an abridged (from 545 to 233 pages) and popularized form – popularized so far as the language was simplified, i.e. made less academic and more American (the original thesis was translated by an Englishman) and thus more accessible to non-academic (including native American, or "Indian") readers. The word "primitive" was taken away and the term "North American Indians" was replaced by "Native Americans". Hultkrantz took part in the changes. However, an error was made: Hultkrantz' name was confused with that of a distant relative of his, who was also a professor, but in a different subject, and at the University of Uppsala, which is why the book cover states: "Åke Hultkrantz is a professor emeritus in ethnology and religion at Uppsala University, the oldest and most distinguished university in Scandinavia." The complete title of the American publication is: *Åke Hultkrantz. Soul and Native Americans. (originally published as Conceptions of the Soul among North American Indians) edited with a foreword by Robert Holland. Woodstock 1997.* For a doctoral thesis this represents a strange fate that, apart from the confusion of names, undeniably signifies appreciation.

7. Paulson 1958.

8. Paulson 1961.

9. Bäckman & Hultkrantz 1978. *Louise Bäckman. Samlade studier i samisk religion. [Studies in Saami Religion. Collected articles written by Louise Bäckman in Swedish and English]* was published as the beginning of Stockholm History of Religions' Centennial Series, Part 1 (The Departments of Ethnology, History of Religions and Gender Studies, the University of Stockholm). Additional parts of this series were planned but unfortunately could not be completed due to lack of funds.

10. Berglie 1983.

11. Here the Canadian visiting researcher Daniel Merkur could be mentioned, who at our department presented his thesis *Becoming Half Hidden: Shamanism and Initation Among the Inuit.* Acta Universitatis Stockholmiensis, Stockholm Studies in Comparative Religion 24. Stockholm 1985 and Åke Hultkrantz' *Shamanic Healing and Ritual Drama. Health and Medicine in Native North American Religious traditions.* Crossroad, New York 1992.

12. It can be mentioned here that when prior to this publication I presented this preface to the department's research seminar, there were

some participants who thought that the great number of concepts of the soul made a slightly ridiculous impression. My response to this is that the last element "-soul" should not be taken too literally. It is a pedagogical term, which is attached to *all* the psychological observations/concepts that *together* constitute the background to the later uniform (monistic) concept of the soul. If the "part" ("-soul") is unreflectingly associated with the "whole" ("soul") of course a certain confusion arises due to the words' power over thought.

13. This reminds me of Martin Persson Nilsson's classic work: *Helvetets förhistoria. Straff och sällhet i den andra världen i förkristen religion* [*The Prehistory of Hell. Punishment and Bliss in the Other World in Pre-Christian Religion*] 1963.

14. Ginzburg 2004; 2013c.

15. Runeberg 1947. Ginzburg refers to this (as far as I can see, in a clearer way than in the English translation) in the Swedish translation of *I benandanti. Stregoneria e culti agrari tra Cinquecento e Seicento, Benandanti. De goda häxmakarna* (1991a, p. 265 f., note 10).

16. Bremmer 1983. This book is an adapted version of the thesis presented at Vrije Universiteit Amsterdam in 1979.

17. For a review of Åke Hultkrantz' field research, see Christopher Vecsey's *Introduction to Åke Hultkrantz. Belief and Worship in Native North America. Edited, with an Introduction by Christopher Vecsey.* Syracuse University Press. Syracuse. New York 1981.

Shamans Emerging From Repression in Siberia: Lightning Rods of Fear and Hope

Marjorie Mandelstam Balzer
Georgetown University, USA

To honor the broad ranging legacy of Åke Hultkranz, this article focuses on the changing social and political ramifications of indigenous people's spiritual revitalization in Siberia. My approach balances Hultkrantz's sensitivity to commonalities of shamanism throughout the circumpolar North with attention to more specific aspects of shamanistic practices and beliefs in Far Eastern Siberia, especially the Sakha Republic (Yakutia), over time. Shamans and shamanic prophets can be found in many kinds of communities, from rural Siberia to Native North America to urban Korea. Over-generalizations behind standard or "ideal type" distinctions among "shamans," "priests," and "prophets" limit our understanding of the richness of shamanic cultural traditions.

Research featured here is based on long-term fieldwork, many return trips to Siberia over the past thirty-five years, and work with the Sakha diaspora. It analyses the resurgence of post-Soviet shamanic healing practices, the organization of an Association of Folk Medicine, and shamanic leadership in an ecology activist movement. Shamans explain that their crucial imperative to heal and protect their clients and communities survived the Soviet period. Shamans and others, by adapting shamanic belief systems, can engage, if not soothe, the legacies of social as well as personal suffering. Yet many shamans were killed or repressed in the Soviet period, rituals were suppressed, and the reputations of shamans have long been ambiguous, depending on whom they protect and how. In socially fraught, crisis-ridden contexts, the personal becomes political. Shamans'

How to cite this book chapter:
Balzer, M. M. 2016. Shamans Emerging From Repression in Siberia: Lightning Rods of Fear and Hope. In: Jackson, P. (ed.) *Horizons of Shamanism: A Triangular Approach to the History and Anthropology of Ecstatic Techniques.* Pp. 1–34. Stockholm: Stockholm University Press. DOI: http://dx.doi.org/10.16993/bag.c. License: CC-BY 4.0

motivations and authenticity are debated. A prophylactic against shamanic misuse of perceived spiritual power is the widespread belief that if shamans use their "helping spirits" for revenge or impure purposes, this can literally come back to haunt them, their families, and their descendants. Contemporary Siberian shamans, some of whom have suffered traumatic, validating spiritual initiations, often find themselves powerless to combat familiar "global" problems such as exploitation by outsiders and increasingly horrific environmental destruction. Shamans become lightening rods of both fear and hope for those who believe in them.

Introduction: Approaches of Åke Hultkranz and Other Classic Views

My first contact with Åke was in 1993 at a conference on shamanism in Budapest, where he was the keynote speaker for the founding of the International Society of Shamanistic Research. He scolded me, as an American, for possibly being among those who do not pay enough attention to European scholarship, especially on Native American rituals and beliefs. I decided he was right, especially after reading the wonderful book he gave me: *Shamanic Healing and Ritual Drama: Health and Medicine in Native North American Religious Traditions* (New York: Crossroad, 1992). Rereading Åke's publications and those of his students, such as Joseph Epes Brown (2007), has deepened my understanding of the early commitment of the University of Stockholm's Department of Religion to an open-minded approach to religious traditions in the broadest sense. That legacy continued with the November 8, 2013 workshop of shamanism.

A significant aspect of Åke's work is brought out by remembering the tension between his search for Northern commonalities of shamanism, including "eschatological conceptions of soul beliefs" (Hultkranz 1953: 7; 1993), in juxtaposition with Jane Atkinson's insistence on shamanisms and shamanship (1989; 1992). Åke was frank about his concern that if we narrowed our studies of shamans too far into emphasis on specific communities and individuals, we would lose sight of what gives us a common vocabulary to study religious traditions that have deep intertwined roots and fascinating philosophical convergences.

I try to balance these two major, competing concerns in shamanic studies, without reproducing Åke's main distinctions between the world views and practices of hunters versus agriculturalists (in the Native North American context). I also tend to "problematize" that slippery word "tradition," since as an anthropologist I have been trained to be very specific about historical context and periodization. Any romantic hope for revealing pristine "untouched" "pre-contact" Native traditions in the 21rst-century, including in a place as seemingly remote as Siberia, should be abandoned.

In the anthropology literature, both classic (Max Weber, Victor Turner) and current (David Hicks, David Gellner) distinctions are often made between religious practitioners with charismatic, idiosyncratic sources of inspiration and those with more institutionalized, regularized and learned sources of authority. These become the "shamans" and "priests" of different kinds of societies, often posited in hierarchical or evolutionary relationships.[1] Shamans are relegated, in some such schemes, to the lowest rungs, to small traditional communities, while priests flourish in complex, urban societies with elaborate social roles to serve globalizing or "world" religions. Mediating these two extremes are the "prophets," who derive spiritual power from creative uses of authority: they are at once charismatic and socially significant. Prophets in such conceptions become those leaders known for energetically forcing their social groups out of seasoned patterns during times of crisis and cultural change, sometimes into new religious movements.[2]

I argue here against the over-generalizations behind these standard or "ideal type" definitions, since shamans and shamanic prophets can be found in many kinds of communities, from rural Siberia to Native North America to urban Korea (compare Kendall 2009; Hoppál 1992; Humphrey 1999). Further, the boundary defying roles of priestly prayer chanters, emergency spiritual healers and charismatic trickster shamans can sometimes be found in the same person. I make my case using data from the Sakha Republic (Yakutia), where I have done periodic fieldwork since 1986. Rather than privileging "outsider" definitions with rigid or "etic" distinctions, I attempt to use the flexible and subtle local "emic" distinctions that Sakha themselves make concerning overlapping kinds of shamans. These are in part, although not entirely, based on various kinds of spirits associated with particular practitioners or actions. Shamans functioning as white-light purifying prayer leaders are described as "*aiyy oiuun*," to stress their connection with benevolent "*aiyy*" spirits of the sky (compare Eliade 2004). Shamans who summon other spirits, through drumming or jaw harp, are termed "*oiuun*" if they are men and "*udagan*" if they are women. Their spirits include those of the earth, *ichchi[ler]*, and a more capricious or dangerous category, "*abaaghy*". The complexities and debated meanings of the relevant terms, beyond healer specialization, are illustrated here by focus on several famed shamans, especially the Soviet period shaman Konstantin Chirkov, who predicted the demise of the Soviet Union; his surgeon daughter Alexandra; the currently revered É'dii (Elder Sister) Dora Kobiakova; and the recently deceased Vladimir Kondakov, founder of the Association of Folk Medicine. Before turning to featured shamans, I also provide narratives of shamanic power, in order to viscerally enable understanding of the ways historical shaman-related events remain salient yet reworked in current conceptions and ritual behavior.

My conclusions stress the need to think beyond the simplistic dualism of "black" (sorcerer) and "white" (priestly) shamans, attributing general evil or benevolent intent to whole specific categories of people without sensitivity to context and change. One family's sorcerer may be another's healer-defender, particularly in situations of competition between shamans. Similarly, we need to transcend worn analytical habits of privileging European, Christian influenced, definitions over local logics. Nuanced local language and belief system complexities can then become the more prestigious analytical categories, opening up new ways to discuss cross-cultural comparisons (Lindquist and Coleman 2008). Rationality is relativized, while acknowledging the salience of mutual influences over multiple generations of post-colonial contacts (Handler 2004).

A more personal confession is perhaps appropriate here. In the post-Soviet milieu of struggling for indigenous people's cultural revitalization, I have felt an ethical, fieldwork imperative to sympathize with narratives of shamans' repressions during the Soviet period and to affirm shamanic reputations for healing. In the Far East of Russia, Sakha Republic (Yakutia), it has been delightful to extol large-scale festivals that open with eloquent "white shaman" prayer-blessings. Yet no researcher with sensitivity to accounts of their interlocutors could fail to notice what has sometimes been called "the dark side" of shamanic power (compare M. Brown 1988; 1989; Whitehead and Wright 2004). I thus concede that it is misleading to dismiss as merely blackening due to the influence of Soviet and Christian propaganda certain indigenous narratives that are frankly chilling. However, listeners should not anticipate murder mystery intrigues. The accounts that follow must be placed within an indigenous cosmological and analytical framework that incorporates diverse shamanic powers and reputations. I claim, along with many Siberians, that reputations of shamans have long been ambiguous, depending on whom the shamans protect and how. For example, indigenous interlocutors circulate morale-building narratives of shamans able to defeat Soviet jailers and atheist propagandists in mystical, socially transcendent ways (Balzer 2012:46–56). Shamanic practices are situational, contingent on political context and community support. Their interpretation is intertwined with "eye of the beholder" issues of cultural relativism, natural relativism and "perspectivism".

Narratives of Shamanic Power: When Spirits of the Past Remain Present

At least in recent periods if not earlier, the chill effect of shamanic abuse of power has probably been outweighed by the beneficial effects of shamanic individual and community healing. Numerous accounts of shamanic initiations throughout Siberia and Central Asia vividly depict being "chosen by the spirits" against one's will and without recourse once "spirit torture" or "spirit illness" begins (Basilov 1997 [1984]). This spiritual road is far too difficult to be chosen lightly. I have collected personal initiation narratives, including convincing post-Soviet accounts that depict healers' resulting abilities to have "radical empathy" with their future supplicants (Balzer 2012; compare Koss-Chioino 2006). For example, the village shaman Vitaly, known for curing alcoholics, and supported by his local government with a special curing hut in the forest, explained in 1997: "Since childhood I have had dreams, horrible nightmares, as I at first thought them. First a bear came to me. With a stuk, stuk, stuk, advancing on me. I was terrified. I would lie awake at night and not be able to sleep, in a sweat... Then other stages followed. I felt I was being torn apart, and then put into a horrible press, with pressure on all sides coming down at me." A thong on Vitaly's neck holds a bear tooth talisman, since the bear has become his *iie kyl*, "mother animal spirit," his main guide into multiple worlds of the Sakha cosmology. In a familiar pattern, Vitaly was healed only after he promised to heal others.

A contrasting sunset-of-life account of shamanic power was confided in 2012 by an elderly woman originally from the Niurba area of Sakha republic about her grandmother:

> "You know that they say when people are dying, toward their end, they lose their shamanic talents? My grandmother had been bed-ridden and blind for several years. She was really sinking and out of it. However, toward the end something very different happened. She got back her spiritual gift, her singing. But it happened in a very scary way. The family could not predict when she was going to die. It was duck hunting season. And my father, my brother and my brother-in-law, three generations, set out for a specific hunting site pretty far away. They had three guns. Grandmother was aware they were gone. She started to sing, a kind of descriptive chant. And my mother's hair nearly stood on end. She was terrified – for what grandmother sang was that three men, of three generations, had shot each other by accident while they were hunting. It was in the same general place that our family had gone, only it turned out to be across the river, this incident. It really happened – but it turned out it the killing was not in our family but another family. We still wonder – had grandmother seen this whole thing, visual-ized it somehow in simultaneous time, and described it so vividly, as if she were there? Had she perhaps averted the tragedy from our family to someone else's? Was she describing or actually influ-encing events? We never found out. She died soon after. I am very scared of this kind of [spirit] power, and do not want it for myself, do not like talking about it...."

We are plunged into a realm of thought and action here that is be-yond the experience of most, and not easily reducible to general-izations about special cognitive talents of "clear seeing" shamans.

Memories concerning this grandmother, and other frightening aspects of the speaker's life history, caused her to turn away from shamans to the New Apostolic church in 1998. Yet her so-called "conversion" has not stopped her faith in shamanic powers, particularly in the Cassandra-like abilities of certain shamans to see, warn of, and sometimes help divert, disasters. Thus her narrative, and many others, can provoke us into thinking more deeply about why and how individuals and communities retain powerful, circulating memories about frightening spiritual worlds, even when they insist they would rather live without such memories and such spirituality. These are far more significant than titillating "ghost stories" (in Sakha *yuer*) told around a campfire. In culturally mixed contexts, especially times of socio-economic crisis, political upheaval, and shifting religious values, spiritual conflicts become exacerbated, as data from across the North and from Mongolia and Nepal, amply reveal.[3] They are too unpredictable and politically contingent to enable generalizations about the decline of violence or the advance of humanism (compare Pinker 2011).

Another blatantly predictive "Cassandra" narrative reinforces my claim that accounts of shamans and spirits are widespread and maintained through indigenous community fascination well into post-Soviet times. Such narratives often depict violent events of the Soviet period. Their current circulation perhaps serves as an ongoing processing of the ramifications of Soviet repression of shamans, given their significance as exemplars and leaders of folk religiosity. I heard this one in 2012 from an interlocutor who prefers to remain anonymous:

> "Zina had special talents from a very early age. She died young and had a very rough life. They [Soviet doctors] said she was schizophrenic, and they gave her drugs to "cure" her. At one point she actually broke a window trying to escape. She died relatively young, in a hospital, age 52, many years ago. Her own mother was an *udagan* [female shaman] or at least a *menerik* [spirit message receiver]. Zina sang... and when she did she could predict trouble, but no one appreciated her. [MMB: As if she was out of Greek tragedy?] Yes, she was like Cassandra. Here is an example. Zina envisioned ahead an accident involving a truck and a motorcycle. She saw that a construction vehicle lost a chain that flew back at a

young man riding a motorcycle behind it, and he was thrown off and killed. She knew that young man, who was handsome, had a good potential future and was just out of the army. So she decided to warn him to be careful on his motorcycle, and she told him what she had seen. But he laughed it off and about a week later he was killed, just as she had envisioned. This was such a freak accident it is hard to imagine it being made up ahead of time. Incidentally, Zina was not a pure Sakha. Her mama was Sakha, and her papa was some sort of Russian/ Polish mix. But the gift for clear-seeing runs especially in the maternal line, and she had it, to her despair."

Zina's tragedy was compounded by Soviet contempt for all who exhibited shamanic tendencies, such as visions. Psychiatric treatment was usually a form of psychiatric imprisonment, with pseudo-doctors in white coats using a debilitating cocktail of drugs to suppress perceived abnormality. They often diagnosed as "schizophrenic" those who defied the Soviet system. Political and religious dissidents were predominant among their victims, throughout the Soviet Union (Grigoryants 1989). The Siberian variation on this theme is that some of the "best and brightest" potential shamans were thwarted in their ability to fulfill what many saw as their destiny. Instead, they became unloved and mocked by their own communities. In hindsight, we might say that not only the young man, but others around Zina would have done well to heed her visions. But they were powerless to do so in the social milieu of the time, and thus they also were condemned to localize the Cassandra legend that literally has resonance from other times and places. Note too that my literate interlocutor named the Cassandra pattern, by definition featuring unloved, thwarted seers. In the Sakha language, a clear-seer is called *keubecheu*, a clear hearer is *yeustachi*, and the idea of telepathy is encompassed in the term *aharas eteei kihi*, glossed as "person with an open body".

A more positive outcome of shamanic power contestation in the Soviet period fits into a set of narratives that valorize shamans. These are legend-like accounts of certain secretly revered shamans who had the ability to transcend and defeat Soviet authorities. For example, this narrative was gifted to me by the ethnographer Semen Ivanovich Nikolaev (penname Somogotto, July 1991) about one of the most famed shamans of the 20th-century, Nikon:

"The young Komsomol activists who were supposed to be arresting shamans were themselves scared of them…. The great shaman Nikon was invited to a club by some Komsomol. They were trying to expose charlatans, and to catch and jail them, confiscating cloaks and drums. So they invited Nikon, and he threatened them… He came onto the stage at the club and said, "If I scare you, will you promise not to arrest or punish me?" They promised. And he raised his arm. There appeared, to the whole crowd, a whole group of bears. There was panic in the hall, but he closed the curtains and smiled: "Remember, you promised, and you said you would not be scared."

Similar stories were told about Konstantin *oiuun*, who also brought bears to a contest with Komsomol workers. But ultimately both shamans were arrested. Konstantin turned himself into a bird in the jail, and could easily have flown away, according to another account. But instead, so as not to get his family in trouble, he just sat outside the jail, returned to human form, reading a book. This was to show he could escape if he wanted to.

Helplessness when caught between political and spiritual powers is a recurring theme. Some narratives reveal direct conflicts between the old and new or between Sakha and Russian values. Examples include the tensions between values of ecological preservation versus development. Impossible choices result, and are sometimes processed as nightmares. This 2012 narrative comes from a Suntar Sakha family, who wish anonymity:

"One aunt was in a line of seers… She was beautiful and married a man who became one of the first Sakha executives at the Mirny diamond mine, in the Soviet period. She had a dream soon after they moved there. An old man, dressed all in white, a white bearded sage spirit of the local region (*doidu ichchité*), came to her and said the diamonds are not for human exploitation. People are not supposed to be digging up the wealth of the earth. This is not for you to just grab. He spoke in a rich Sakha language, filled with poetry. She wrote his archaic words down and showed them to me later. They were beautiful words but he also threatened: anyone taking these diamonds will come to harm."

After I asked whether Russians too were targeted, my interlocutor explained that the spirit "does not distinguish nationality." She grimly added that a Russian woman geologist, who had helped find the Mirny vein, had died an early death and that others also came to bad ends, mostly Russians and Poles, since they were predominant. The frightened aunt had told her husband about the dream, but they could do nothing about it. Indeed, "they had trouble, first with having children, and then with premature death in the family." Her own son died young and they attributed it to the threat. They eventually were able to move away.

Sakha guilt and grief at the devastation caused by open pit mining should not be underestimated. It is reflected in this amazing dream, where the relevant spirit is far from "evil," but rather is the ancient "white" elder- keeper of the whole region (*doidu ichchité*, literally glossed as homeland middle-earth spirit). Recently a daughter in the family unexpectedly married an engineer, who was assigned back to Mirny. Her mother, thinking "oh no, not again," gave her daughter strict instructions to "feed" the local spirit of Mirny, through a fire, an offering of nearly an entire bottle of vodka. Since the daughter's Sakha language was poor and colloquial, her mother wrote a suggested model prayer (*algys*) with appropriate words. The gist of the prayer, to be improvised in the daughter's own words when she was fully, spiritually ready and humble, was that the couple had moved to Mirny against their will, were planning no harm to the earth and its local spirit-keeper, and that they wished to have a fertile, successful family. Several months later, the anxious mother confirmed that her educated, Russified daughter had indeed appealed to the local spirit, although she had never done anything like it before.

While the open diamond pit at Mirny, one of the world's largest, is exhausted, other veins nearby have been discovered, and industrialization continues at an alarming pace, as far as many Sakha are concerned. They have become a minority in their own local region of Mirny, and are in danger of becoming politically powerless. Many resent recentralized federal relations, exemplified by Russians taking over the Sakha diamond company ALROSA as President Putin came to power. At a partially compensatory spiritual level, bridging Soviet and post-Soviet periods, Sakha have for many years told stories of early deaths coming to mostly Russian developers, especially of roads that disturbed Sakha graveyards. All this, as well as a recent pipeline perilously close to the Lena River, provides context for a major ecology movement in the

Sakha Republic, partially led by a shaman-turned-activist Éd'ii Dora, discussed ahead.

A lesson some of my interlocutors derive from emerging spiritualities is that one does not have to be a shaman to use shamanic powers. Indeed it said that those who do not know how to use the powers properly, to show appropriate spirit respect, are those who most often get burned. This is one reason why Afanasy Fedorov, an actor-turned-healer, stopped using the exact wording of certain trance-inducing seance prayers. He confided to me that he did not want to go beyond his perceived ability to control his spirituality. He sensed his own limits, at the threshold of the spirit world, beyond which he feared falling into a trance and never waking up. His account relates to a well known Sakha saying, that words themselves have "spirit," *ichchi.*

In sum, many shamanic narratives have become "morality plays," reinforcing belief systems and community behavior or norms. A strong, probably archaic belief, sometimes reinforced by whispered rumor to this day, is that when shamans use their powers to cause harm, those ill deeds can literally come back to haunt them in the form of harm to themselves or deaths among their loved ones. This is a powerful deterrent against abuse of spiritual power. But community-based defensive morality leaves room for shamanic revenge against those perceived to have become enemy others, including "ethnic others". Thus shamanic narratives have become a valorizing, compensatory way of interpreting memories of Soviet repression. Contemporary fears of alcoholism at personal levels, and ecological destruction at community levels, are relatively recent forms of pollution that shamanic spiritual prowess, oriented toward purification and social-ecological balance, can potentially address, if not fully heal.

Shamans and their Legacies

Konstantin and Alexandra: Adapting "the healing gift" to fit the times

One of the most celebrated shamans of 20th-century Siberia was Konstantin *oiuun.* His masterful cures, personal integrity, and quiet community leadership centered on his ability to tap into what the

Sakha term *kut-siur*, or a combination of heart-mind-soul-spirit. Accounts of his secret healing practice in the Soviet period have become popular in the post-Soviet period among his many grateful patients, and through the memoirs of his daughter, Alexandra, with whom I have worked periodically since 1992. Like many trickster shamans throughout the circumpolar North and beyond, he used healing humor during his seances and he shrewdly knew who among his supplicants would respond well to his efforts. In 1993, one of his assistants, Maria Ivanovna Rebrova, then in her eighties but a young (pre-menstrual) girl when she helped him, regaled me and her close family with descriptions she had kept secret for decades:

> "In Arlakh, one woman had a psychological illness. Konstantin was invited. She had been sick for a long time... Again I warmed the drum by the fire, and his clothes, and got everything ready, especially the *dépsé* (white horse skin). He started to dance. Well this sick woman had on a red dress and was completely bedridden. He was dancing furiously. All of the sudden, the red dress was outside – not on her body but walking outside along by itself, without any person in it. So the *abaaghy* [capricious spirit possessing the woman] was sent away in the dress. And Konstantin kept dancing."

Maria's family (and I) dissolved into laughter at this story, which was, according to Maria, even funnier at the time. The woman was discretely slipped a new dress by the end of the seance, at which time she had "completely recovered". Laughter therapy as well as Konstantin's dialogue with the *abaaghy* was undoubtedly part of the benefit of this seance.

Whether they used momentary inspiration, bawdiness or "speaking in tongues," shamans could not produce a fully effective or satisfying seance event unless they were known for spiritual depth and humbleness. Within their own cosmological-philosophical systems, shamans were and are respected as wise spiritual advisors and keepers of a huge range of sacred knowledge, not just religious ballet masters, crazed prophets or charlatan actors. In Sakha reasoning, a truly powerful and effective seance performance is the mark of spirituality, revealing the ability to bend flexible levels of reality to one's needs. In other words, the medium gives the message of spirituality and power.[4]

Konstantin's daughter, Alexandra Chirkova, at his urging became a Moscow-credentialed European-style medical surgeon, and the head doctor of her northern region. After age fifty, she returned to the shamanic healing traditions of her father, incorporating spirituality into her therapies selectively and creatively, depending on the patient. In the past decade, Alexandra has commuted between her home in the town of Belaia Gora, and the capital of Sakha Republic, Yakutsk. In Yakutsk, she has worked in several "traditional" healing centers, usually without using her father's inherited cloak or drum. She briefly treated the former Sakha Republic president, Mikhail E. Nikolaev, before he left the presidency, enhancing her reputation.

In childhood, Alexandra had notorious symptoms of shamanic illness, called in the Sakha language *éttétén* and "the Sakha sickness" [*Sakha yld'ybyt*]. A form of "spirit torture," it often results in painful feelings of being "sick all over," of being torn apart and remade from the inside out by snakes and other animal-like spirits. One goal of this "initiation" is to feel a variety of pains that one's future patients are likely to feel, to gain enough empathy to become a true intuitive healer, tapping into the spiritual potency of oneself and one's patients in a synergistic way. To recover, a potential healer must promise to cure others, in a literally and figuratively enlightening bargain with spirits who become one's helpers.[5] Alexandra explained to me: "I was young when I first felt the strength. I had visions, forebodings. But I was also headstrong and emotional... Father tried to tell me this was not how to be. I had a dream that I was thrown into a pit with snakes. I heard a voice that said "She will see it through. She will win.""

Alexandra, confirming that various stages of transformation are typical of Sakha shamans, describes a later episode in her memoir (2002:100–106):

"In 1985, something happened with me that is beyond explanation. It began with a headache and unstoppable vomiting. For three days, I was not able to get up from bed, and then I revived. The whole time I wanted fish... My body was covered with red hives. I had a terrible skin itch, as if worms were crawling all over my body... A woman came to me and said that I was not curing myself correctly, that what I had was well known... After feeling better, I decided to take the smell of [her incense] from my body. But again the headaches began, and I realized that I must put on my father's cloak... I put it on and immediately ... felt a tranquilizing of the soul; with a great yawn I lost my footing, and fell into a deep dream...."

After taking sick leave, Alexandra continued to use her father's cloak to cure herself, as she gradually realized that what was happening was "the ritual of tearing apart". She explains this as "a ritual of suffering through which one is taught". Among the teachers were animal spirit guides, including a bear. Significantly, one of Konstantin's most famed forms was as a bear, his "mother animal spirit". Her suffering was far from over. She would sing ancient Sakha songs with abandon in her sleep, awakening her confused husband. And after three years, a trauma occurred that led her away from being "the kind of doctor who cuts and sews," as her father used to say. After performing a brain surgery, she reeled from the operating room, vomited, was unconscious for three days. Fearing inappropriate drug treatment, she landed in several hospitals, including in the republic capital, Yakutsk. Gradually, she realized: "I had acquired a new gift, the ability to see through a person into their illness." She saved one woman from a kidney stone operation by willing the stones into sand. Another, who was to have a leg amputated, was saved when Alexandra "by thought, with intense gaze, cured her. Soon she stood, felt warmth, and itching in the leg." As she cured others, she improved herself, and was finally released, still wobbly, with the diagnosis "sickness uncertain".

Back home, donning Konstantin's cloak, Alexandra finally felt relief and calm that led to her spiritual transference from a surgeon to a healer, guided by the spirit of her father, who sometimes sent messages through an elderly mediator fondly named "Aunt Shura". Within ten years, Alexandra resigned as head doctor, and began receiving selected patients in her home, including those she helped occasionally by donning Konstantin's cloak and drumming by a fire, in a special healing hut in her back yard. Alexandra is well loved for dealing with emergencies, with the traumas of hunting accidents, as well as for curing nervous system disorders and alcoholism. Nikolai, a patient with cancer, and several others, have said that they see a man standing behind her while she chants, as she evokes the beauty of the Northern mountains.

Éd'ii Dora and Vladimir Kondakov: Emerging Spiritual Leadership

In 1999, the famous mummy of a Sakha woman-*udagan*, who had spent the Soviet period in the Yaroslavsky museum of Yakutsk, was ceremonially reburied in the Megino-Kangalask region. Acting as a psychopomp (escort of spirits) and prayer leader, Fedora Innokentievna Kobiakova, respectfully called Éd'ii Dora, led the ritual. Dora's ritual included a cow sacrifice, with parts of its meat scattered to ravens. Dora implored local Sakha not to hunt or trespass near the grave, but one man shot a goose nearby and his daughter died soon after. Dora had warned that the awakened spirit, unsettled and readjusting, might take small or even large sacrifices. Several other deaths, including a child of five with cancer and a boy of nineteen who committed suicide, were attributed locally to the reburial. Later that same year, on the day I passed a full two kilometers from the burial, a small bird (chickadee) died before my eyes, and a horse was killed, bizarrely caught in downed telephone wires. Friends with whom I witnessed these deaths correlated them to Dora's warning about possible sacrifices.

The lesson was double-edged: stirring up dead souls (*kut*), especially of shamans, can bring disaster; but appealing to shamanic ancestors with proper ritual respect can bring rewards. Sakha today often are afraid to literally unearth a grave or uncover a tree-platform *aranghas* where dead shamans reside. But metaphorically, they are searching for buried affirmation of many possible identities. While some are grateful to be free of shamanic heritage, others selectively rejoice in it. Shamans, curers, artists and scholars today sometimes return to the resting places of particular famed deceased shamans when in critical need of spiritual guidance.

The historical shamans they appeal to had many functions, characteristics and personalities. They were rarely seen as solely "white" or "black" in their motives or their communication with a range of spirits. Rather, like Dora, their trouble-shooting actions were appropriately based on particular tasks, whether leading a life-crisis ritual, purifying during a seasonal ceremony, putting out a forest fire, calming the waters of a flood, negotiating disputes, curing the ill with myriad techniques, and much more. In each case, the fire spirit (*iot ichchi*) was and continues to be the crucial entrée into other cosmological worlds, whether during summer solstice *yhyakh* ceremonies or small private seances involving travel to the spirit world.[6]

Both male and female shamans were and are said to move through different levels of skill over their lifetime. Local scholars debate whether one or the other genders was stronger historically (compare Balzer 1996; Tedlock 2005). Shamans usually begin as *kuturukhsut*, helpers, but if this is not possible their apprenticeships can be guided by the spirits who have called them to service. Shamans then progress through various informal ranks. In Sakha social expectations, lesser *oiuun* or *udagan* are likely to practice blood letting, bone setting and predictions of the future. At this stage, they should have at least one helping spirit. Middle level *oiuun* or *udagan* have a greater range of skills, and a greater number of helping spirits, acquired through spirit journey trances to both upper and lower worlds of the complex Sakha cosmology. Great *oiuun* or *udagan*, who have always been rare, have wide reputations for knowing myriad techniques and controlling numerous animal and other helper spirits.

Dora (born in 1959) has told the Sakha ethnographer Ekaterina Romanova (2008: 315) that she has been passing through the stages mentioned above, growing in her spiritual strength, since age 12. A crucial year for experiencing intense bouts of the "shamanic illness" was age 30. As with other spiritual leaders in Sakha conceptions, her strength was further enhanced after age 40, when people feel freer to reveal their full creative potential. By numerous accounts, she has reached levels of success beyond her abilities to cure individuals, becoming a leader in a contemporary, fledgling movement for the moral, spiritual, and ecological healing of the Sakha people and lands. Tall and imposing, with a round, kind face and long hair, Dora looks the part of an Earth Mother-Priestess. She has acquired numerous mediator spirits for different purposes and different kinds of cosmological contacts, including birds (swan, crane, cuckoo, loon, woodpecker) for the upper world, elk and bull for the middle earth (*ortu doidu*), and bass and duck for the watery underworld. She is a real mother, a widow with shamanic heritage from the Kobei region, whose curing "miracles," celebrated anomalies, have become as renowned as her impassioned speeches and mass rituals using lovely archaic Sakha prayer-blessings. Her clients and admirers are legion, including the former President of the Republic, Mikhail E. Nikolaev. Dora has become so well known that few healer-purification leaders in the republic are considered her equal.[7]

Dora has described how she heals in revealing interviews with an admirer, Nina I. Protopopova ([2003] 2006), although Dora also has said that she has trouble explaining in words her techniques and the requirements of being "chosen by Nature" to heal people.[8] Dora's helper-spirits, especially the "mediating birds" swan and crane, reveal who will visit her and whose bones she should use to suck out illness. She also trouble-shoots through dreams and intuitive perceptions at dawn. More profoundly, she taps into the natural interconnectivity of humans, flora and fauna. Each human when born is linked in spirit to a gendered tree and an animal, often a bird, living in that person's homeland. "This is my system. Those who come to me for cures have a special protection that derives from their land and their kin [ancestors]." Dora empathetically uses the "energy" of that connection to restore health, if necessary by flying:

"When I raise myself, I stand straight and go where I am needed. What is traveling is my energy. My vision along the way depends on natural circumstances. Across destroyed earth, I can fly as wind or fog. Over more calm rivers and lakes, I reacquire my own self. I can go anywhere, whether Viliuisk, Japan, America... my body is at home, but my energy is moving [like smoke from a cigarette] to where it is needed, and then returns."

One family took their daughter out of the best Yakutsk hospital when doctors said they could do nothing for her brain tumor without a risky operation. The girl was fading, hardly able to lift her head or to see. They traveled far to Kobei, where Dora used a hollow bird bone to suck out the illness (*sullerdeen*) and gradually return her to health.[9] The girl later attended a university. Dora also uses six drums (*dungur*) of three sizes, with the two largest reserved for special natural or human emergencies. She more often uses three consecrated wooden spoons (*khamyiiakh*) of birch, pine and larch, decorated with special symbols, for predictions and help with purification of patients. In addition, she has sacred jaw harps (*khomus*), three for curing and one for communing in nature.

Individual shamanic cures, no matter how sensational, constitute neither a movement nor proof of what Edith Turner (1999) calls the collective subliminal, revising Jung (1926), and playing on Victor Turner's (1977) concept of ritual "liminality". But Dora's language, her claims, and her recent rituals suggest correlations of her philosophy of Sakha cultural renewal with major Sakha shamans of the past and with other Native prophetic spiritual leaders who founded new religious movements for their struggling peoples.[10] After flooding of the Lena River in 1998, Dora proclaimed in mass meetings: "The spirit of the earth warns us with fires and floods that we must embrace Nature, that we must not forget that we are Sakha. Nature is giving a signal that each *ulus*, each *nasleg* (subdistrict) should not appeal to others for help but should themselves generate their own beneficial renewal." Although some Sakha have blamed Dora for not predicting the Lena River floods, she in retrospect looked on the flooding as punishing purification of Sakha sins:

> "Nature has eyes, a bellybutton, and roots, veins. The spirit of our great earth has east, west, north and south sides, with a strong foundation. We, the Uranghai Sakha, created strong, were born on that very place that the spirit of Nature built his hearth. We are designated to live in harmony with Nature... yet we, despite considering ourselves a wise people in preserving our language and history, have violated the behests of Nature, and for that sin are being punished. Nature, insulted, has responded with the bitter tears of a flood."[11]

Like many Sakha, Dora considers that a key to healing the Sakha people and their land is the reverent summer celebration of *yhyakh,* preferably on the bank of a river or lake, or on a rise with a great vista. While the republic declared June 21 an official holiday soon after it declared sovereignty within the Russian

Federation in 1991, debate continues over the profanation of the festival in Soviet and post-Soviet times. Dora urges return to the original meaning of *yhyakh*, as a ritual stimulating fertility of people and land, as well as seasonal, cyclical balances of Nature. The summer solstice, when people are closest to Nature, is Nature's day of peak flourishing and purification potential. "One should go to the soil of one's homeland on that day, take horse meat shashlik and fish, milk products and pancakes, or even just tea, and sit on the green grass in the circle of one's own kin and friends at the sacred *yhyakh* place (*tyuhyul'ge*)."[12] As Dora explained to Ekaterina Romanova (2008:320), "We must always honor the sun, and during *yhyakh* we must be especially thankful, for in the summer all nature is awakened and all spirits are alert."

Contemporary young Sakha women sometimes fault Dora for being too "traditional," too worried about sexual "sins," and too oriented toward women's roles as wives and mothers, encouraging large families. But Dora advocates higher education for all, including her own daughters. Her advice to young parents stresses the need to stimulate all children to study well, as well as to be proud of traditions of cattle and horse breeding. Scolding, cursing, and disharmony, she reminds, were always discouraged in Sakha families. To avoid the scourges of alcoholism and poverty, so rife in Sakha villages, she suggests trying to help children find value in any kind of labor, whether paid or not. Sakha were once self-sufficient, without money, and need not today find meaning in life only through outsider- or state- driven employment.

Dora is no revolutionary, but she does have social messages that she repeats in meetings and interviews, addressed to her own people. Others should not be blamed for Sakha problems, she suggests, even though as a people Sakha may be as much as fifty years behind where they might have been, both morally and economically, without Soviet rule. "With other peoples one should have an open heart and good will. But at the same time, one should not allow inconsiderate behavior." She adds: "It is not in the nature of the Sakha people to protest, demonstrate and act out." For survival, Sakha have become cautious. Elders who participated in war and experienced starvation should teach young people the perils of interethnic and inter-community disharmony.

Dora's messages jive well with her times, and she is popular in villages as well as in some corridors of power. Through Andrei Savich Borisov, the Minister of Culture, she has been hired to bless major *yhyakh* ceremonies, as well as the openings of new theaters and sports stadiums. Dora does not call herself either an *oiuun* (reserved for men) or an *udagan* (a female shaman) but rather lets her admirers do that for her. She openly describes flying to other worlds, and her lovely, archaic blessings help validate her powers and the very existence of spirits for her followers. Her strong poetic prayers, kindness and obvious commitment to ecological activism have made her an enduring presence in the republic. And yet Dora herself has been frustrated in translating her ecology movement into a new level of intelligent, sustained development. She continues to plan a substantial community center/clinic on the outskirts of Yakutsk, but she has thus far been functioning without a major infrastructure to support her curing practice and larger purification program. Her campaigns to save particular sacred places, such as the whole Tuimaada Valley where Yakutsk is located, have been unable to withstand government plans for development of gas and oil pipelines and the first rail line into Yakutsk. They have been unable to prevent gas pipeline accidents that have occurred at the Lena River near Olekminsk. Political and economic forces "higher" than Dora, or the Ministry for Protection of Nature (Ytyk Kéré Sirér in Sakha), or any other ecology activists, have stymied the possibility that shamanic connection with Nature could make an important contribution to the health of all the republic's peoples on the scale that is needed.

Dora is a contemporary example of a combined shaman-priest-prophet. She is "priestly" when she leads purification prayers, shamanic when curing the ill, and prophetic when foreseeing the trouble that comes from reconnecting with spirits of dead shamans. Significantly, she considers herself the reincarnation of one of the most revered and legendary shamans of the 19th-century, the beautiful Alykhardaakh (also called Alykhyrdaakh), whose spirit helper-avatars were a bass and a loon. Sakha who know her well and revere her poetic language believe in her reincarnation identity. Thus she bridges worlds of contemporary and past Sakha spirit mediation at a crucial moment of crisis and hope for her people.[13]

Vladimir Alekseevich Kondakov was a tall, heavy-set, lightly-bearded man of fifty one when I met him in 1991. He was already well known as a curer and a prayer-singer, having moved from his home region of Viliuisk to the capital, Yakutsk. He had dropped an official career as an historian and school teacher to pursue his shamanic, spirit-guided destiny (*d'ylgha*) with an openness that had not been possible in the Soviet period. When he died in 2009, an outpouring of respect and sorrow for his passing was evident in the circles of curers, artists and patients who had relied on his wisdom and healing talent. In the broader, government-controlled Sakha press, his legacy was mentioned in a more muted way. While this may have derived from the complexities of his personality, it probably had more to do with visible retrenchment of enthusiasm for shamanic healing in the past decade. However, his Association has survived his death, and his own life, in retrospect, seems to illustrate my arguments concerning the overlapping and situational nature of shamanic roles and significance.

Over the years from 1991–2007, I periodically visited the Association's several clean, sparsely decorated clinics. Vladimir's office was adorned with portraits of shamans, including the famed Nikon of Viliuisk, and his shaman-mentor Igor Gerasimov. I also saw displays in huge bottles of "passed" kidney stones, and observed use of acupuncture as well as shamanic therapies. Patients seemed pleased, although interviewing them on the spot was awkward. By 2009, the Association's website listed many successes, although problems persisted concerning payment for services and members' dues to the Association.

Vladimir, in the last decade of his life, consolidated his Association of Folk Medicine into 75 members including 5 shamans, moved its headquarters, wrote many books and novels featuring shamanic healing, and performed in concerts with his wonderful, sonorous, booming voice. Some joked that one ancestor may have been a Russian Orthodox priest, since his singing persona seemed to evoke Christian spiritual style. He was proud that an ancestor, the *aiyy oiuun* "white shaman" Tumus Mékhélé (Mikhail Pavlov), had in 1897 blessed a new Orthodox church in the Viliuisk village of Khampa. His last interviews, and his Association website, constantly stressed his "benevolent spirit shaman" identity, as did his obituaries, for example one mixing Sakha and Russian in its title: "Vladimir Kondakov Aiyy Shaman has Left Life". He had a degree in psychology and was a licensed hypnotist, to help legitimize his Association. Through the Association, he also promoted respect for nature, for Sakha "ancient spiritual traditions," and for Sakha family values. The Association's long list of curing services continues to include "incantations for phases of the planet," and enlistment of help from "the cosmic strength of [Sky God] Aar Aiyy and benevolent earth spirits [*ichchiler*]". In a 2004 interview, he rather sensationally implied that he, as a true *aiyy* shaman, could go beyond the 9th Sky level (where branches of shamanic trees end) to reach the "tenth, eleventh and twelfth heavens" in an emergency.[14]

Vladimir, at my urging in 1991, discussed the basic goals of his Association: "to establish, study, and put into practice the best traditions and methods of Sakha curing". He stressed that a wide range of traditional Sakha specialists had operated before the Russian revolution, and that as many as 14 different kinds of doctors, or more accurately categories of doctoring, had existed in Sakha communities before the arrival of the Russians in the 17th-century. They included the purifying *algyschit*, or prayer and incantation specialist; the *otohut*, or bone-setter and herbal specialist, from the root *ot*, meaning grasses; the *kuturukhsut*, or shaman's assistant, who literally helped the shaman not to fall into the fire during trance; the *ilbiihut*, or massage ritualist; and the *ohko keurteurkheueuchchu*, or elderly midwife, from the phrase "lifting the child out". Each had continued practice secretly in Soviet times, but often in losing competition to Soviet doctors.[15]

For Vladimir, the goal of the rich Sakha shamanic "philosophical system" was to try "to balance forces of the three worlds, and of evil and good." To help people live in proper balance within the middle world, our earth, powerful shaman-mediators must be able to communicate with spirits in nine levels each of the upper and lower worlds. The directions East and West also represent a balance between middle world forces of good and evil. Thus, the West may be where relatively dark forces (*abaaghy*) emerge from the underworld and the East correlates with relatively benign forces (*aiyy*). Vladimir perceptively claimed: "The danger today is that the middle world is destroying itself, and the balances are out of kilter." Shamans must therefore creatively use the *abaaghy* and *aiyy* to reset the balance, to correct local ecological problems, find lost objects, predict the future, see into the past, or to cure an ill patient.

On the debate over whether shamans can be divided into "white" (benevolent) and "black" (malevolent) categories, Vladimir wisely taught that "few shamans are purely white or black, today or in history." He insisted purely black shamans were especially rare: "Most shamans are mixed in the forces they use and in their purposes. They themselves must feel the balance. If they do evil, they will be punished themselves. An evil shaman will be judged at death. This is not only in Christianity. All of nature punishes people who are evil. The Sakha person has always tried hard not to do evil or truck with evil. Sakha are frightened of *sét* [retribution]. This was not their Christianity; this was before Christianity" (cf. Troshansky 1903).

Vladimir nonetheless considered the "white shaman" a key to the history of the Sakha people, and a legacy of their roots in Turkic and Mongolic cultures farther south. In this, he was following popular Sakha ethnographers (compare Alekseev 1984; Romanova 1997), who claim that the Sakha originally had only white shamans, but gained more evil-doing "black" shamans from neighboring Evenk (Tungus) influences, after Sakha ancestors traveled north. Vladimir's view of black shamans was more complex and personal, but he too speculated:

"The white shaman was governmental. He was the leader of his tribe. He opened the *yhyakh* festival with *algys*. He performed white shamanic rituals in service of the cult of the Sky God Uluu Aiyy Toyon, and he was the messenger of this greatest of Sky Gods. He cured, but this was not the main issue. He advocated when to go to war. He was skilled in diplomacy. He predicted the weather; he knew how to save his tribe in emergencies. He was the main advisor to whomever was the main tribal leader, if he was not this leader himself. The first shaman was probably white. His power was from Uluu Aiyy Toyon. But the black shaman was local. Not because he was evil did he become a black shaman, but perhaps because of tragedies and suffering in his life that he tried to counteract. Perhaps a white shaman had hurt him, and he turned to darker powers for help."

In the last twenty years of his life, Vladimir became known and in demand for his dramatic leadership of summer solstice ceremonies, chanting his own prayer-blessings based on a combination of ancient formulae and improvised poetry. He told me in 1991 that his connection to nature was affirmed for him in a magic moment during a Namsk region *yhyakh*, when he led a large, enthusiastic post-Soviet crowd with the opening *algys*:

> "I addressed the spirits, by chanting with prayers, without my drum, as a white shaman would. I was connecting with the Earth by pouring *kumiss* to her, by a fire. Then I connected with the spirits of the sky, by tossing *kumiss* to the Great Upper Sky God. And suddenly rain came, just in the area where we were, gentle and not for long. We brought rain to the village. Nature, all of Nature, listened. I saw this. I felt this."

Vladimir compensated for the pain and sacrifices that he made as a Sakha shaman, including the rumor-producing death of a talented daughter, with a sense of mission and balance with multi-dimensional nature. One of his *alygs* was broadcast when he died in 2009:

> Supreme God Urun Aar Toyon looking with magnanimous eyes,
> Always protect; with clemency, good calling,
> Our Body-blood strengthen, cure, brains educate,
> Heads, our brain's every "fiber", long veins of blood vessels clear,
> Protect my soul filled with light, preserve my dark breath,
> Award with a long life, with opened opportunities
> Let life in our Homeland-Middle world be long lasting,
> Breath endure! Happiness-well-being come to us!
> Generations continue in posterity! Domm! Domm! Domm!

Here, protection of multiple generations by the benevolent Highest Supreme God is accessible through eloquent respectful pleading of the *aiyy oiuun*. In Vladimir's published book of *algys*, he distinguishes prayer-blessings exclusively for the *aiyy oiuun* to speak and those for ordinary people. The *aiyy oiuun* addresses the Supreme God again in the following *algys*, this time acknowledging (as in many of the major monotheistic religions) that His true name can only be said in metaphor (Kondakov 2005: 12–13):

First we praise your great name.
We call you, though your true name is hidden from us!
We see that our families, our ancestors stand behind you!
We beseech you: Bless our young
Bring the power of the Aiyy to bless our people (*aimakhtaryn*) Sakha
May the bright sun shine and protect us, Give us life
May the souls of our life-force (*kut-siur yhyllan*) not fail
May we be protected, so that the lies coming from the breath of
     the lower world spirits be not raised to us, in the Middle World!
May we be protected, so that our *Iié Kut* (mother-soul) in each of
     us be well and strong,
May we be protected, so that we fall not into ill will or illness,
May we be protected, so that all that is evil or capricious passes us by,
May we be protected, so that the *Buor Kut* (earth-soul, material-soul)
     may be strong as an epic hero and may grow,
May we be protected, so that the *Salgyn Kut* (breath-soul) can
     brightly flourish,
     like the sun,
     like a beautiful sunrise,
     like copper, glowing and sparkling in the light,
Let it cover [us] in protection,
... Let not the strong words of an enemy reach out to discourage us,
Let no such evil words reach their mark,
Do not let those who curse come near,
So that no one can offend,
So that the kind breath of understanding, of the *Aiyy*, will be
     everywhere.
Let Our Great People Live and Be fertile in the Middle World!

This world-view revealing *algys* is notable for its lovely convergence of individual and group health, protection and purification.
The three major souls of the Sakha person are explicitly named,
as Åke Hultkrantz would have appreciated. The concept of "our
people" (*aimak*), using a word that connotes both community and
kinship, is significantly emphasized. Potential threats are named,
but so is the calming grace of a beautiful sunrise.

Courting personal spiritual experience is not typical of standard
portrayals of Siberian shamanism, in which a shaman resists the
call of the spirits until given little choice. Rather, it is closer to the
vision quests of North America. Kondakov's exhortations represent his democratization of shamanic sensitivity and worldviews

for contemporary Sakha cultural values. He tapped into a yearning for spiritual fulfillment prevalent in post-Soviet Siberia by reaching deep into what he perceived to be past traditions. When he urged followers to fly to upper worlds, it was meant to be more than metaphor, becoming also a means toward the goal of helping his people out of a spiritual void and physical-ecological devastation. He continued this trend by publishing his easy-to-carry guide to *algys* that included prayer-blessings for ordinary Sakha to say to one another, invoking *aiyy* but not the Supreme Deity, for example before traveling (Kondakov 2005: 16–17).

In sum, Vladimir Kondakov managed to balance between institutionalizing shamanic practice with his Association of Folk Medicine and creating space for personal, creative spirituality. His democratizing of spiritual practice had roots in Sakha rituals of familial prayers to the fire spirit in home hearths and around hunters' campfires. But in the post-Soviet context, his imposing presence and his own charisma provided credibility for shamanic spirituality on a new, Sakha-nation-wide scale. He thus joined Éd'ii Dora in being an exemplar of a combined priest-shaman-prophet.

Black, White and Grey: Shamanic Power, Morality and Multiple Beholders

These narratives and cases of recent shamanic charisma should convince most skeptics that shamans and shamanic concepts are alive if not well in Siberia. Russian developers have died prematurely. Interlocutors who have "converted" to Christianity are convinced their grandmothers were psychic and might exert influence from beyond the grave. Some have attempted to escape shamanic heritage or curses to no avail, despite emigration. Theorists of memory remind us that it is as much about forgetting as remembering, but here are cases where attempts to forget are unsuccessful.[16]

What is it about shamanic worldviews and spirituality that are so lasting yet pliable? They are probably lasting because they are pliable. The sweeping and audacious comparisons of Carlo Ginsburg (1991: 14–18, 136) show potential structural and symbolic correlations of Eurasian shamanic communities across vast swaths of time and space, but they also reveal the importance of understanding the social contexts behind witchcraft accusations against those who thought they were protecting their communities. Definitions of shamans and shamanism continue to be pliable into the twenty first century. My working definition is that shamans are mediators of spirit worlds for a purpose. In its creative folk wisdom, Kondakov's depiction of a balanced cosmological multiverse, where doing ill can backfire onto one's loved ones, is a shamanic variation on significant 20th-century psychological insights, especially those developed by Carl Jung, Otto Rank, and William James, as well as others associated with transpersonal psychology. Correlations between shamanism and expanded understandings of human potential or flexible realities have been made by others.[17]

Particularly analytically challenging are correlations of shamanic abilities and actions with Friedrich Nietzsche-like "perspectivism," in the sense Brazilian anthropologist Eduardo Viveiros de Castro uses it (1998) and Danish anthropologist Morten Pedersen (2011), working in Mongolia, has developed it with the concept of natural relativism. If shamans have the ability to harness or become one with their spirit being "helpers," then they can shift in their cognitive perspectives from hunter to hunted, curer to supplicant, human to animal, human to god. Their multinatural horizons are theoretically infinite, and potentially empathy-based, as is their far-from-simplistic philosophy, long caricatured as "animism".

We can relate this philosophy back to issues of historiography, and the theme of shamanic morality. Despite the literature, we should probably stop imagining early European-contact Siberian and Amazonian shamans as among the most vicious on earth. Christian authorities, missionaries and shamans slandered each other, and this was reflected in our historical records of shamans, filtered through the eyes of missionaries and colonists.[18] Analyzing ramifications of changing social dynamics shed further light. Far from being capriciously amoral, or chameleon in their behaviors, shamans have long lived within socio-political communities in constant flux, subject to great risks, and coping with the consequences of their indigenous groups frequently being driven from their original homelands. This included Mongolic-Turkic ancestors of

Sakha shamans, who probably traveled North with their ragged and devastated families from an original homeland around Lake Baikal before European contact (Gogolev 1993). As leaders who were among the most intelligent and prescient in their communities, shamans of each succeeding generation often became the first fulcrums bearing the brunt of change, including pressures from other communities (warfare), against the environment (development) and against their worldviews (missionaries). This is why Michael Taussig (1987:237) called shamans the "shock absorbers of history". But as their reputations have become tarnished, their ability to engage, negotiate and mitigate change is compromised, and they are plunged into crises of internal dissent and authenticity. Returning to contemporary Siberia, this is precisely what happened to Vladimir Kondakov as he fought in the past two decades to establish his Association of Folk Medicine. It is, however, an institution that has survived his death, probably because the credibility of spirituality and shamanic empathy has begun to be accepted again openly in Sakha society.

This credibility can be seen as socially and politically grounded, defying easy generalizations like "shamans are the poor-person's psychologists". One pioneer of Siberian shamanism-as-group-therapy was Sergei Shirokogoroff (1935). But during his pre-Soviet fieldwork living with Évenki, shamanic nomadic communities were relatively in-tact, albeit under Russian Orthodox siege. Communities that have lived through the Soviet period are in an exponentially different level of chaos and debate over what "traditional values" to preserve, and how to handle spiritual resurgence, seen from human points of view as both situationally welcome and unwelcome (voluntary and involuntary). Some curers have grown into their "called by the spirits" shamanic illness initiations with grace and creativity, such as my friend the accredited doctor and shamanic healer Alexandra Konstantinovna Chirkova. Some seers reputedly have managed to influence juries in court cases or find lost bodies for police departments. But others, especially those who are not shamans but retain some shamanic perspectives, have experienced social, political and economic insecurity along with intensified fears of uncontrolled shamanic heritage, ancestral cursing and revenge that can span generations.

The hallmark of current Sakha spirituality is a chaotic experimentation, an eclectic grasping for meaning in post-Soviet times of trouble and transformation. Myriad ways are being discovered or rediscovered to express Sakha-ness or to go beyond conceptual borders of ethnonational identity into global identities, including literal emigration. But the fieldwork I have been doing with members of the Sakha diaspora in comparison with Sakha remaining in their homeland-republic reveals ongoing, not diminished, shamanic worldviews. More accurate would be to depict a layering of beliefs and practices, situational and filled with disconnects, as is typical for so many 21rst century humans struggling to re-find and re-define communities. If we do not have rationality or consistency in our own faith practices (Wuthnow 2007), why should we expect it in others? The intertwined, systematic aspects of shamanic cosmologies and moralities may be fraying, making it perhaps more appropriate to discuss diverse "faiths" rather than full-blown systematic beliefs or coherent epistemologies. Just as theorists have "unpacked" and dissolved the idea of holistic culture and ethnic group psychological cohesion, we can do the same for holistic religiosity, including shamanism.

Along with this eclecticism comes the need to analyze ideas of competing "authenticity" (Brown 2003; Handler 2004; Marcus, Clifford 1988). Believing in ancestral and other spirits is no more a "badge" or requirement for self-identifying Sakha than is believing in the main God, Aiyy Urung Toyon, of the Sakha Turkic hierarchical cosmology. But when Sakha wish to say with pride that their shamanic philosophies are just as sophisticated as those of ancient Greece or modern Europe, and just as worthy of being called a Religion as Christianity, then they evoke that complex cosmology. Some insist that their elaborate "functional" system of Gods is relevant to their lives today, especially the moral framework that gives those Gods enforcement "teeth". Significantly, Sakha linguists have been active in the revival of Sakha shamanism as a system of spirit and God enforced morality by legitimizing ancient Sakha terms and concepts long discarded. Their "new/old" system has a label, *aiyy yoreghé* (white spirit teaching), taught in republic post-Soviet schools until recently (Afanas'ev 1993). And they have established a center, called *Aiyy Diété*

(Spirit House) on the outskirts of Yakutsk. As anthropologists, historians, or ethnographers, who are we to question newly reconstructed relevancies?

Further implications of valorizing the "white shamans" bring us to inter-indigenous politics. While I can understand the motivations of Sakha scholars and others for differentiating their kind of shamanism from that of other Northern peoples (such as the Éven, Évenki and Yukaghir), we do not have the kind of archeological record that can confirm sharp "ethnic based" differences in sacred ideologies and social organization. Turkic, Mongolic, Tungusic and other peoples mixed over long periods in Northeastern Siberia (Gogolev 1993). Thus it is likely that their cosmologies (pantheons of gods and spirits) and beliefs (ideas of the soul and concepts of reincarnation) have become mutually reinforcing, combined chaotically if not integrated syncretically. For me, a Christianity-derived, "outsider" term like "priest" is an unwarranted imposition onto early Sakha society, although the Russian term *zhrech* may come closer (compare Kharitonova 2006: 328). While it may be prestigious for some to view the *aiyy oiuun* as a kind of priest, it also may hint at a neo-colonial, social hierarchy habit of mind.

For Sakha spiritual legacy, I prefer to stress the freer, creative, flexible, wise trickster-cultural hero shamans, some of whom happened also to have priestly learning and prophetic talent (compare Hyde 1998). Indeed, it is often more useful to analyze changing, contextual relationships over time rather than social roles with sharp "social organizational" definitions. This also may help us worry less about sharp distinctions between "belief systems" and "religions" (compare Siikala and Hoppál 1992). The theology implied in Sakha terms is complex: for example to predict something from observance of patterns (*bilgésit bilgé*) is different from foresight derived from a deeper intuition (*but tangha*), or from being able to prophecy destiny (*keubiue'chiu d'ylgha*).

Sakha may compare themselves to ancient Greece or modern Europe, or to other indigenous groups. Some anthropologists of Latin America, including those attuned to indigenous worldviews, epistemologies and ontologies, have termed new indigenous activism plus self-awareness "emerging indigeneities" (Fortun et al

2010; de la Cadena and Starn 2007). They celebrate the perspectivism and multinaturalism mentioned above, and this has been adapted by French iconoclast Bruno Latour, famed for his recognition of internal dissents captured in the concept of "iconoclash" (Latour 2002; 2009). Without becoming caught in their distinctions between "epistemological" and "ontological" thinking, I see the greatest relevance for any reborn valorization of shamanic credibility to be in constantly asserting that responsible indigenous caretakers should have legal rights to their homelands and subsurface minerals on a human rights basis. We can then entertain the possibility that shamans and their followers may have special ways of seeing the natural-human connectivity nexus that further validates those rights and renders especially urgent our understanding of human potential, community orientations, and deep ecological knowledge. This is what makes the Native American spiritual rights activism of George Tinker (2004) and the synthetic, engaged approaches of Canadian scholar Paul Nadasdy (2007) enormously appropriate. As indigenous authorities, they epitomize new generations of what Åke Hultkrantz (1983: 107) meant when he wrote: "It is most urgent that those involved in religious research among American Indians evince *Einfühlung*, respect the Sacred, and try to read its meaning. In so doing, they enhance the importance of their research as a contribution to the history of religions".

Throughout their turbulent histories, empathetic shamans, using all the senses they could muster, have perceived and tried to sooth the messy, changing legacies of intertwined personal and social suffering. In the process, shamans have become lightning rods of fear and hope for those who believe in them.

Acknowledgements

I am grateful to the University of Stockholm's Department of Ethnology, History of Religions, and Gender Studies, and especially to the organizers and participants of the symposium "Horizons of Shamanism: A Triangular Approach" November 8, 2013. This article also owes much to the generosity of Sakha (Yakut) friends and colleagues, to Georgetown University, and to the U. S. National Endowment for Humanities.

Notes

1. Compare Weber ([1922]1963), V. Turner (1972), Hicks (2010), and D. Gellner (1994). Victor Turner (1972: 437–444), influenced by Max Weber, William Lessa and Evon Vogt, differentiated priests and shamans: "a shaman's powers come by 'divine stroke,' a priest's power is inherited or is derived from the body of codified and standardized knowledge that he [sic] learns from older priests... Shamanistic rites are 'noncalendrical,' or contingent upon occasions of mishap and illness. The priest and priestly cult organization are characteristically found in the more structurally elaborated food-producing – usually agricultural – societies, where the more common ceremonial is a public rite performed for the benefit of a whole village or community". David Hicks (2010: 133), in his reader on religion, continues this traditional interpretation: "Like priests, shamans mediate between spirits and human beings. Unlike priests, though, shamans usually require to a pronounced degree that personal quality known as 'charisma' in their personality." However, our Western "folk conceptions" of the best priests also include the idea that they should be both "charismatic" and have "a calling". See also Narby and Huxley (2001).

2. Literature on new religious movements is vast. See for example Daschke and Ashcraft (2005); and Rob Nanninga's bibliography (2002) www.clas.ufl.edu/users/gthursby/rel/nanninga.htm. For Native American revitalization, see especially Hultkrantz (1997) on the Peyote "cult," Mooney (1991) on the "Ghost Dance," and Wallace (1972) on the "Handsome Lake movement".

3. See, for example, Carpenter (1961); Buyandelger (2013); Pedersen (2010); Riboli and Torri (2013).

4. This is similar to the "reality of spirits" argument that William Lyon (2012) makes in his controversial book *Spirit Talkers* on Native American medicine powers and their correlation to theories of quantum physics.

5. Compare Basilov (1997); J. Brown (2007); J. Brown and Cousins (2001); Hultkrantz (1992); Mehl-Madrona (1997).

6. For perspective on Sakha cosmology, see Afanas'ev [Téris] (1993); Alekseev (1984); Bravina (2005); Gogolev (2002); Kolodesnikov (2000); Ksenofontov (1992); Kulakovsky (1979); Romanova (1994, 1997); Yakovlev (2000). On repressions, see Vasil'eva (2000).

7. I met Dora in 2000 and 2004, and talked with her without formal interviews, including one memorable exchange at a summer solstice ceremony in the Taata region when I made the mistake of gesturing toward a large cricket-like bug that had landed on her chest, to the horror of a mutual friend. My friend was concerned that the bug was Dora's and my gesture was disrespectful. Dora seemed more amused than annoyed. I have been collecting stories about her for years, and hope to work more closely with her.

8. Quotes are mostly from Nina I. Protopopova's interviews. I am also grateful to the National Institute of Health doctor Lev Goldfarb, who gave me a film that he made of Dora's healing techniques with her commentary.

9. This "sucking cure" is similar to techniques of Native Americans, for example as featured in the California Indian films "Sucking Doctor," and "Pomo Shaman," produced by William Hieck, 1964, available through University of California Extension Center for Media and Independent Learning, catalogue numbers 37454 (original), 37439 (edited).

10. Especially relevant is the Native American (Handsome Lake) spiritual revitalization that Anthony Wallace (1956, 1972) long ago called "goal culture". Compare Wallace (1956: 265); Nagel (1997); Balzer (1999); E. Turner (2006).

11. Compare Protopopova (1999: 177–178) and the more generalized Russian translation of Protopopova (2006: 59–60).

12. The passage acknowledges that each community may celebrate *yhyakh* in its own way (Protopopova 1999: 186–7). This alleviates pressures that some indigenous ethnographers have put on communities planning the celebrations to follow specific ritual details.

13. On Native American reincarnation, compare Hultkrantz (1953); Mills and Slobodin (1994).

14. For this interview with Irina Efimova "Belyi Shaman Vladimir Kondakov" see www.dvmusic.ru/index/articles/one/full/1517 (accessed 7/20/09). See the Association's website www.aaraiyyitegele.ru/index_rus.php?id=1&i=56 (accessed 7/20/09). An obituary also appeared in the Sakha parliament's online journal "Vladimir Kondakov Aiyy Shaman has Left Life" at www.v-yakutia.ru/?id=11984 (accessed 7/20/09).

15. See Kondakov (1992, 1993, 1997, 1999). See also Senkina (1991).

16. See for example, Criukshank and Argunova (2000) on the Sakha Republic; Grant (2009); Ricoeur (2004).

17. The thesis that shamans use their own full range of psychological potential while stimulating individual and community health has been stressed particularly well by Krippner (2000), Csordas (2002), and Tedlock (2008). Romanucci-Ross (1977) pioneered in correlating interrelationships between body/mind healing and the "body politic". Practitioner-scholars Lyon (2012) and Harner (2013) emphasize the flexibility of non-ordinary reality.

18. See also Balzer (1999; 2012); Flaherty (1992); Znamenskii (2003); Narby and Huxley (2001); and Tedlock (2005). Compare Willerslav (2007).

Travelling in Spirit: From Friuli to Siberia

Carlo Ginzburg
UCLA, USA and Scuola normale superiore, Pisa, Italy

1. I never met a shaman in my life. My knowledge of shamans
and their European counterparts (if they ever existed: an issue
I will address later) is unashamedly bookish. But should I really
be ashamed? Isn't history an honorable craft, which more often
than not deals with books and papers, old and new, preserved in
libraries and archives?

These rhetorical questions will lead us nowhere, unless we assume that both historians and anthropologists share an experience of distance – the distance between the observers' categories
and those of the actors.[1] I am referring to the well known distinction between *etic* and *emic* levels of analysis that Kenneth Pike,
anthropologist, linguist and missionary, picked up and reworked
from linguistics (*etic* and *emic* referring, respectively, to phonetics
and phonemics). As I argued elsewhere, Pike's argument might
be rephrased as follows: observers (including historians) ask *etic*
questions which are either anachronistic or ethnocentric, or both,
in order to retrieve, through a long and sometimes difficult trajectory, *emic* answers – the categories and voices of the actors.
Far from identifying a scientific approach with either the *etic* or
the *emic* (as Pike and Lévi-Strauss did, respectively) I have argued
that historians and anthropologists should engage in a sustained
dialogue between the two dimensions, *etic* and *emic*.[2]

2. The dichotomy between observers' and actors' categories will
provide a framework for the case study I am going to share with
you: a retrospective evaluation of my own research experience over
thirty years, from the early sixties to the late eighties, from my first

How to cite this book chapter:
Ginzburg, C. 2016. Travelling In Spirit: From Friuli to Siberia. In: Jackson, P.
(ed.) *Horizons of Shamanism: A Triangular Approach to the History and
Anthropology of Ecstatic Techniques.* Pp. 35–51. Stockholm: Stockholm
University Press. DOI: http://dx.doi.org/10.16993/bag.d. License: CC-BY 4.0

book (*I benandanti*, translated into English as *The Night Battles*) to *Storia notturna. Decifrazione del sabba*, translated into English as *Ecstasies. Deciphering the Witches' Sabbath*. As a student back in 1959, I made a triple, sudden decision: to become a historian; to work on witchcraft trials in early modern Europe; to focus on the attitudes, beliefs, voices of the women and men accused of witchcraft. The latter decision had both biographical and ideological implications: on the one hand, my memories as a Jewish child during the Second World War; on the other, my recent encounter with Antonio Gramsci's Prison Notebooks, written in the Fascist prisons. I had been particularly impressed by Gramsci's remarks on "the culture of subaltern classes" (*cultura delle classi subalterne*). But my project to approach witchcraft trials as a crude form of class struggle was also a deliberate updating of Jules Michelet's romantic vision of the "Witch" as a symbol of social revolt.

A document, dated 1519, I found in the Inquisition files preserved in the State Archive of Modena, seemed to provide support for my initial hypothesis: a trial against a peasant, Chiara Signorini, accused of having cast a spell against her landlady, who had ejected Chiara from her own possession. But in the essay (the first I ever published) dedicated to that trial I ultimately pointed at a broader issue, i.e. the cultural clash between the inquisitor and the peasant woman. "Cases such as that of Chiara Signorini" I concluded "can have exemplary value even in their most unique aspects". [3] The word for "exemplary" in the original Italian version – "paradigmatico" – did not imply an allusion to Thomas Kuhn's paradigm, since *The Structure of Scientific Revolutions* was published the year after: but the tension between cases and generalizations was already at the heart of my research, where it has remained ever since. I will come back to this issue later.

3. The inquisitor who conducted Chiara Signorini's trial was the Dominican friar Bartolomeo Spina, the author of a well known demonological treatise (*Quaestio de strigibus*). May we describe him as an observer, who relied upon psychological and physical pressures to convince Chiara to answer his own questions – his own *etic* questions – following his lead? If we were to accept this implicit analogy we might also note that Chiara withstood the

Inquisitor's pressures on one matter only: she stubbornly refused to confess she had taken part in the witches' Sabbath. May we say that the latter element was not part of Chiara's *emic* categories?

A long time ago I began to work in this direction in an essay entitled "The Inquisitor as Anthropologist".[4] A reversal of the analogy – "The Anthropologist as Inquisitor" – would stress the concern for truth, as well as the cultural distance, shared by both anthropologists and inquisitors vis-à-vis the actors they were confronted with (i.e. natives, defendants). But as soon as we look at those asymmetrical relationships from a distance, everything becomes more complex: both observers and actors would turn into actors. For instance, the observer I was at that time would become, in the eyes of the observer I am now, an actor. Let me add immediately that I am not particularly attracted by the fashionable notion of agency. Acting, or acted upon? I am tempted to answer this question in Latin, echoing (with due qualifications) Martin Luther's famous dictum: *actus, non agens*. As you will see, the multiplication of egos I will deal with in my presentation does not have a narcissistic purpose – quite the contrary.

4. The unexpected feeling of disappointment I experienced in discovering a document which seemed to confirm my initial hypothesis – witchcraft as a crude form of class struggle – had left me without a specific research program. I spent one year (1963) wandering across Central and Northern Italy, searching for fragments of Inquisition archives and reading as many witchcraft trials as I could, at random. One day, while I was consulting the Inquisition trials preserved in State Archive of Venice, I came across a testimony given in 1591 by Menichino, a young cowherd from Latisana, a little town in Friuli. He said that, since he was born in a caul (that is, wrapped in the amniotic sac) he was a *benandante* (literally, somebody who goes for the good): therefore, he was compelled to dream, three times a year, to go "like in a smoke" in the field of Josaphat, where he fought with fennel stalks against the witches, "to preserve the faith". Then he added: "when the benandanti won it was a sign of a good harvest". The dream (Menichino explained) first came to him after a conversation he had had with a friend, Giambattista Tamburlino, who had also declared he was a *benandante*. "When you have to come, you

will come" Tamburlino said. "You will not be able to force me" Menichino replied. His friend insisted: "You will have to come anyway". "And a year after these conversations", Menichino went on "I dreamed that I was in Josaphat's field".[5]

In an essay I wrote many years ago I tried to reflect on the reasons for my own excitement in coming across that document – a discovery that led me to write a book on 16th- and 17th-century Friulian benandanti.[6] I was astonished at the amount of unexpected details which emerged from those documents, unveiling a deep layer of peasant beliefs. As I told in my book, the Inquisitors tried to fill the gap between what they expected and what they heard from the benandanti, urging the benandanti to confess that they were not counter-witches at all but real witches. But in my retrospective reflection I refrained from explaining (first of all, to myself) why an analogy between Friulian benandanti and Siberian shamans had struck me as being self-evident almost right away. I will address this issue now.

5. In Andrei Znamenski's helpful book on the impact of shamanism on the Western imagination, I have been enlisted among the scholars who felt the impact of Mircea Eliade's "cross-cultural and transcendental vision of shamanism".[7] "In fact", Znamenski remarked, "in his essay *Some Observations on European Witchcraft* (1975) Eliade had already pointed to the similarities he had noticed between witches' practices described in European folklore and shamanic trances".[8] In fact, in that essay, as any reader (Znamenski excepted) can see, Eliade started from my own book (published in 1966) to advance parallels between Friulian benandanti and Romanian *calusarii*, as evidence of his earlier argument about shamanism as a broad, cross-cultural phenomenon.[9] I will leave aside my strong reservations about Eliade as a scholar, which I have expressed elsewhere.[10] Here I would like to point out that when I first came across the benandanti I had not read Eliade's writings on shamanism. What I knew about shamanism came from another, far more original source: Ernesto de Martino's *Il mondo magico*, published in 1948, later translated into seven languages.[11]

The impact of de Martino's book on the English-speaking world has, so far, been minimal.[12] This may be partly ascribed to a scandalously inadequate translation, first published in 1972, after the author's death, and then reprinted several times, with the title *Primitive Magic: the Psychic Powers of Shamans and Sorcerers*.[13] In this English version the introduction, as well several passages and footnotes, were tacitly suppressed; some quotations were tacitly added; above all, de Martino's highly nuanced, peculiar style was grossly simplified, to the point of distortion.

I will say something about de Martino's complex work and personality in a while. But first, let me point out that shamans play a crucial role in *Il mondo magico*, as its very beginning – a two-page long quotation from Sergei Shirokogoroff's *The Psychomental Complex of the Tungus*, published in London in 1935, a book which, as you know, has remained a classic reference on shamanism until today.[14] Let me take a short passage from that quotation:

> "In the state of great concentration the shamans and other people may come into communication with other shamans and ordinary people. (...) The shamans use this method in their common practice when they want to meet some people or other shamans. Sometimes they do not realize the motive as to why they leave one place or go to another where they meet the person who called them – 'they go because they feel they must go'." [15]

This passage must have crossed my mind as soon as I read the dialogue between Tamburlino and Menichino, the two benandanti from Latisana: "When you have to come, you will come". Their conversation worked as an initiation, anticipating – and apparently producing – the specific content of the dream Menichino had one year later. (Later, I found detailed descriptions of initiations and dreams in dozens of trials against Friulian benandanti). If at that time I had had direct access to Shirokogoroff's book, I would have found more parallels. For instance, the following passage, which de Martino skipped in his quotation from the aforementioned text:

> "...before falling asleep the Tungus express their desire to see distant places and people. If the dream occurs the fact is interpreted as a voluntary direction of the soul".[16]

6. In the nineteen sixties my knowledge of Shirokogoroff's ethnographic work was still mediated, and filtered, by de Martino.

I mention this seemingly irrelevant detail in my attempt to recon-struct a chapter in the historiography of shamanism, conceived as a case study in the transmission of knowledge. An experiment in intellectual history, perhaps? Yes, but even more an experiment in the history of reading – an activity shared today by a large part of the human kind, but still inadequately analyzed in its complexity.

The relatively simple case I am dealing with implies a chain of transmission based on three links: (a) Shirokogoroff's *Psychomental Complex of the Tungus*; (b) de Martino's reading of that book (which he first reviewed, and then quoted extensively in *Il mondo magico*); (c) my indirect and partial access to Shirokogoroff's book through de Martino's *Il mondo magico*. In principle, in order to understand how the chain worked one should focus on each of its links. The limits of my knowledge (first of all, linguistic) prevent me from dealing adequately with Shirokogoroff's truly impressive work, which I have only recently read. But something should be said about its theoretical framework, and especially its anti-ethnocentric attitude, duly pointed out by Andrei Znamenski in his detailed comment.[17] But "anti-ethnocentric attitude" is a mild label for Shirokogoroff's radical relativism. His sarcastic references to "European folklore" included medieval cosmogonies, 19th-century evolution theory, and ultimately "science" (in telling quotation marks), as in the following passage:

> "...cosmogony of the Middle Ages is already fixed as medieval folklore, regardless of whether it was created by the most learned scholastic scholars or by the ignorant farmers. We may say that the theory of evolution with its teleological background as it was practiced, professed, in the European universities in the middle of the 19th-century, in the eyes of the present generation being styled as a 'scientific theory', in the eyes of later generations will appear in its real form of European folklore of a given period. (...) The basis of this attitude is a strong belief in the difference between 'science' as knowledge of realities and method, on the one hand, and 'folk imagination' crystallized in 'folklore' (in the common sense)."[18]

Shirokogoroff's dismissive remark on the theory of evolution and its teleological background had a self-critical implication. A few years before he had put forward a theory of ethnos according to which:

"The division of mankind into the ethnical units (ethnoses) is a natural function which is at the same time an impulse of development of man as a whole" and culture "is a product of a purely biological function, and all phenomena of a physical, social, psychic and technical order are concrete manifestations of this process".[19]

In *The Psychomental Complex of the Tungus* ethnical units still play a central role, although Shirokogoroff explicitly rejected traditional racist theories as:

"confined only to phenotypic rough characters, such as forms of the head, body, limbs and hair, also pigmentation, while perhaps the most important characters, the chemical functional complex and physical constructive complex remain beyond observation, without speaking of the chromosomes and plasma, about the differences of which in human species we have only vague guesses".[20]

Shirokogoroff could not foresee that in a few decades Luigi Cavalli Sforza and other geneticists would have demonstrated that within the human species there are no significant genetic differences. But Shirokogoroff's commitment to scientific progress (like in the aforementioned passage) apparently implied a distantiation from his early positivist background. In a footnote (Shirokogoroff often used them for methodological digressions) he commented on the "ambiguous term 'objective'", remarking that a "philosophical" discussion" about it:

"nowadays would be quite superfluous for no abstraction of the thinking process is possible, the process being physically bound with the cognizing individual and all his cognition is a mere reaction of the milieu. (…) When I oppose 'objective' to 'subjective' I have in view only a relative elimination of rude feelings and now quite evident theoretical aberrations which are still prevailing in the young sciences".[21]

Shirokogoroff's radically *emic* approach (to use Kenneth Pike's categories once again) must be interpreted in the light of those passages. His painstaking ethnographic accounts of shaman practices were fuelled by a scornful reversal of traditional ethnographic assumptions. "Folklore" was science, and science was "European folklore". Nowadays, the shocking overtone of the following remark could easily be missed:

> "In so far as the shaman uses his intuition in the 'finding of causes' he does not differ from any other man who is using the method of breaking of the existing ethnographic complex as a means for proceeding from the known to the unknown". [22]

In a previous passage Shirokogoroff had written "The Tungus have many "facts" supporting their hypothesis" about *ojan*, i.e. spirits. [23]

In reading a statement like this I am tempted to compare *The Psychomental Complex of the Tungus* with another book also published in 1935, in Basel: Ludwik Fleck's *Entstehung und Entwicklung einer wissenschaftlichen Tatsache (Genesis and Development of a Scientific Fact)*, made posthumously famous by Thomas Kuhn in his *Structure of Scientific Revolutions*. For the time being, I am unable to say whether Fleck's and Shirokogoroff's radical relativism could be regarded as similar developments from a common source.

But coming back to Shirokogoroff: is a purely *emic* approach possible? The answer is no. Shirokogoroff himself once wrote: "As a matter of fact, we have only one method which may be used, namely, the comparative method" – a sentence which might have inspired Evans-Pritchard's famous gloss "and that is impossible". [24] Comparison necessarily implies an *etic* point of view, which for Shirokogroff coincided with his theory of ethnos – probably the most problematic element of his work. Although he changed his view about them, he took ethnic units for granted.

7. De Martino owned a copy of *The Psychomental Complex of the Tungus*, published a review of it in 1942, but was already extensively quoting it in 1940. [25] What brought Shirokogoroff's book to his attention was, presumably, another book mentioned in *Il mondo magico*: Wilhelm Mühlmann's *Methodik der Völkerkunde*, Stuttgart 1938. [26]

Mühlmann, the author of a well known history of anthropology went through a long and successful academic career in anthropology and folklore; two bibliographies dedicated to him after the War duly included his earlier books on *Rassenkunde* (he was a full-fledged Nazi).[27] In his *Methodik* – in many ways a remarkable book – he repeatedly mentioned, and warmly praised, *The Psychomental Complex* as an example of accomplished functionalist anthropology, based on a historical and psychological approach. Moreover, Mühlmann advanced some challenging comparisons between Shirokogoroff's *Psychomental Complex* and another book, recently published: Gregory Bateson's *Naven*.[28] In an obituary, published in 1940, Mühlmann included long passages from letters sent by Shirokogoroff (who died the year before) from his exile in China in the late '30s: violent anti-British tirades, cautious appreciation of the political developments in Germany, insightful self-reflections on *The Psychomental Complex of the Tungus*.[29]

De Martino may have come across that obituary: but his interest in Shirokogoroff's work was located elsewhere. In a long article, the first part of which came out in 1942 (it later became, in revised form, the first chapter of *Il mondo magico*) de Martino objected to the customary skepticism, shared by almost all ethnologists, concerning the reality of magical powers among "primitive" populations. This scandalous issue should be seriously addressed, de Martino argued, on the basis of parapsychology and related phenomena, which he had been deeply interested in since his youth.[30] In this perspective, de Martino quoted long passages from *The Psychomental Complex* as evidence for the reality of magical powers among the Tungus. The "facts" that Shirokogoroff had recorded in detail, driven by the cognitive imperatives of his radical relativism, were inscribed by de Martino in his own, very different, perspective. Let me say right away that I do not share (and I never did) either de Martino's interest in parapsychology or his attempt to demonstrate the reality of magical powers. But I was (and I am) deeply interested in the bold theoretical argument which de Martino advanced in *Il mondo magico*. Here is a highly compressed, and necessarily inadequate, presentation of it.

Today we are used to taking reality for granted, along with our presence in it: but this, de Martino argued, is the outcome of a long historical process, in which magic played a crucial role. As one learns from accounts based on ethnographic fieldwork on different cultures, human beings, when confronted with highly critical situations, are threatened by a "loss of presence" – the risk of being submerged in the world. (Once again, de Martino was relying upon Shirokogoroff's work on the Tungus, especially on what he called "olonism" – a compulsive mimicry of other people's behavior). In those critical situations the shaman acts as a cultural hero, reestablishing the human presence in the world. The shaman's performance is a relic from an unrecorded past. *Il mondo magico* is a bold attempt to retrieve this past – a layer which took place before history, making human history possible.[31]

Needless to say, de Martino's argument is entirely speculative.[32] But until recently I was not aware of the deep emotional overtones of de Martino's reading of *The Psychomental Complex of the Tungus*. They emerge in Giordana Charuty's fine biography of de Martino, based on a large number of unpublished documents: *Les vies antérieures d'un anthropologue* (The Former Lives of an Anthropologist). In his youth de Martino had suffered from epileptic seizures, which he reinterpreted, retrospectively, in the framework of his own concept of "loss of presence":

> "The experience of epileptic 'aura' is the sign that presence is going to weaken... [After the crisis] presence re-emerges from the shipwreck, along with a world which has retrieved its forms, its feelings. It was like sliding down from history, slowly".[33]

In de Martino's *Il mondo magico* we can easily detect – today – a strong element of conscious personal identification with the shaman and his world. Shirokogoroff's approach appealed to de Martino not only for its intrinsic intellectual value, but also for its rejection of earlier pathological interpretations based on "arctic hysteria". By turning European science into European folklore, and the shaman into a cultural hero, Shirokogoroff paved the way for de Martino's interpretation.

8. *Il mondo magico* gave me an indirect access to Shirokogoroff's work on Tungus shamans, as well as a powerful interpretive tool: de Martino's "loss of presence". Both elements affected my response to the testimony of Menichino da Latisana, which I stumbled upon in the Venice State Archive. I discovered more Inquisition trials, in which male and female benandanti talked

at length about the battles they used to fight in spirit, usually four times a year, against witches, for the fertility of the crops. Later, in the introduction to my book, I wrote: "I have not dealt with the question of the relationship which undoubtedly *does exist* between benandanti and shamans" (in the Italian version I had written, even more bluntly, "esistente", existing).[34] A stab in the dark, which many years afterwards I decided to turn into a research project.

Its outcome– *Storia notturna*, translated into English as *Ecstasies: Deciphering the Witches' Sabbath* – has been hotly debated.[35] I will not attempt to retrace the trajectory which led me to argue that the image of the witches' Sabbath emerged from the convergence between an aggressive conspiratorial stereotype and a deep layer of shamanistic beliefs. I will limit myself to making some comments on the most debatable element of my book: the attempt to rely on a dual approach, morphological and historical.

What ultimately led me to morphology was my distrust vis-a-vis shaman*ism* as a transcultural category. If I had accepted it, the analogy between the Friulian benandanti and Siberian shamans, which came to my mind at the very beginning of my research, would have found an immediate, and seemingly legitimate, explanation. My attitude was different: the analogy, I thought, implied a connection which I felt unable to address. From an historian's point of view, the question I was confronted with was inadmissible.

I wandered for a couple of years, reading extensively, without a definite plan, reading works of different kinds on witches and shamans. Then chance once again befell my path. While I was visiting the Archaeological Museum in Siracusa, I was suddenly struck by a detail of a huge Greek vase representing a battle of the Amazons, which reminded me of a similar detail in a fresco by Piero della Francesca in Arezzo. I decided to commit myself to a completely new project: research on Piero, which ultimately became a book dealing with some of his works.[36] Many years later I realized that such detour into art history unconsciously addressed the problem I was grappling with in my research on the witches' Sabbath: the relationship between form and context.

Piero della Francesca's pictorial trajectory is a much debated topic among art historians, due to lack of chronological evidence.

I tried to circumvent the obstacle by focusing on contextual elements (iconography and patrons) which suggested a chronology that significantly diverged from the one advanced by art historians, based on stylistic data. To address the analogy between benandanti and shamans I made a similar experiment, but in reverse: I used a morphological approach which led me to put forward a plausible historical context. As I explained in my book *Storia notturna*, I was especially inspired by two imaginative developments of Goethe's morphology: Vladimir Propp's work on folktales and Ludwig Wittgenstein's reflections on "family resemblances".

9. My work on witchcraft has been harshly criticized, among others, by Willem de Blécourt, who has written a few essays on it. Let me quote a passage from one of them, concerning *Storia notturna*:

> "These far-reaching conclusions are based on an analysis that is vaguely structural, profoundly phenomenological, only morphological in name and hardly historical; it is selective instead of serial and devoid of contexts. (…) How can one put history back into a linking exercise based on superficial resemblances?"[37]

Each of these strictures – "selective instead of serial", "devoid of contexts", "superficial resemblances" – deserves a specific discussion. Let me start from the latter, which goes back to morphology. I will briefly mention two pieces of evidence which convinced me that the Friulian benandanti were not an isolated phenomenon. The first is a trial which took place in Livonia at the end of 17th-century. The defendant, an old man named Thiess, confessed he was a werewolf. Three times a year he would go with other werewolves, in the form of wolves, "beyond the sea", in hell, to fight the witches for the fertility of the harvests. We, the werewolves (Thiess said), are "the hounds of God", and our souls ascend to God. Likewise, many benandanti said that, metamorphosed into animals, they fought the witches for the faith and the fertility of the crops.[38] The second piece of evidence – Freud's famous case study on the "wolf-man" – provided me with a further link between benandanti and werewolves: according to Slavic folk beliefs, people born in a caul (i.e. wrapped in the amniotic sac) were supposed to become werewolves. The "wolf-man", Freud's patient from Russia, was born in a caul: a detail that Freud recorded, without realizing its meaning in folk culture. The dream which marked forever the little Russian child – wolves sitting in the branches of a tree and gazing at him – should be regarded, I argued, as a sort of initiation, shaped by the folktales he must have heard from his *nianja*. "The wolf-man's fate" I remarked "differed from what it might have been two or three centuries earlier. Instead of turning into a werewolf he became a neurotic, on the brink of psychosis".[39] A conclusion that Shirokogoroff (I realize now) would have immediately subscribed to.

It would seem hard to dismiss the convergences I mentioned as "superficial". None of the traits involved – and even less their combination – are obvious. But they are certainly related to anomalous, not to say unique cases. According to de Blécourt, *Storia notturna* "harbours a dimly concealed north Italian and even Friulian bias". The reason for the alleged "Friulian bias" are given by de Blécourt himself a few paragraphs later, in a comment to my first book, *I benandanti*: "[it] contains an elegant and well considered presentation of surprising material which is still unique in a European witchcraft context".[40] Unique it was. Retrospectively, I realize that I started from a chance event, an anomalous document (Menichino's confession found in the State Archive of Venice) turning it into a case, first Friulian, then Eurasian. (Incidentally, both terms – case, chance – share the same Latin etymology: *cadere*, to fall).

Here comes de Blécourt's second criticism of my approach, which he labelled "selective instead of serial". But I will not waste your time in rejecting the naive idea that only a serial approach would be appropriate to human sciences and humanities.[41] I used clues – selective clues – in order to build up an experiment which was, as experiments always are, based on a selection of data. Contextual evidence was not part of the experiment. Hopefully, some further research will use it to confirm, to rework or to refute my argument concerning the long term continuities across the Eurasian continent.

According to de Blécourt "the concept of continuity not only provided the framework for the contextualized details which plague *Storia notturna*; it is also one of the foremost articulations of nationalist proclivities".[42] I wonder whether this remark insinuates that I am either an Italian or a Friulian nationalist. "Ginzburg" de Blécourt wrote "never seems to have discovered the fascist leanings of the Romanian historian of religions Mircea Eliade, whom he quotes favorably in *Storia* [*notturna*]".[43] In the footnote related to this remark no references to my book are mentioned. Apparently de Blécourt missed a footnote in which I had written: "The pathos of defeat inspired Eliade, who had behind him a Fascist and anti-Semitic experience (...) to construct a theory of the flight from history" [in his book *The Myth of the Eternal Return*].[44]

10. I will not insist on the aforementioned allegations, which I regard as personally offensive (and false). But they touch upon a very important issue – the political overtones of the debate on shamans and shamanism – which de Blécourt addresses in simplistic terms. The involvement of scholars with a more or less explicit Fascist and Nazi orientation is well known. Their political and ideological commitment usually affected their research – both their approach and their results. But we must bear in mind that (as I once wrote about Georges Dumézil's work) a sharp distinction should be drawn between questions and answers. Answers that we regard as morally or politically unacceptable should not necessarily imply a dismissal of the questions they allegedly addressed. "Even racism, to take one extreme example" I argued "is *one* answer (scientifically unfounded and with a monstrous practical outcome) to a very real question related to the connection between biology and culture".[45] The topics we are discussing, and the scholarship related to them, are full of treacherous, disturbing implications. Political correctness will not protect us.

11. When I first read *Il mondo magico* I was unaware of Shirokogoroff's political orientation; I was unaware of de Martino's personal involvement in relying upon Shirokogoroff's argument; I was aware of de Martino's attempt to demonstrate the reality of magical powers – but I didn't share it. The mixture of conscious and unconscious elements, biases and chance, I have been trying to describe, is not the exception but the rule. All our decisions are taken in a context which is more or less similar to the one I am describing. We are all acted upon and are acting at the same time. Reading can be regarded as a miniature model of all kinds of social and cultural processes – including the intricate

transmission, based on tales, rituals, and dreams, which I have tried to explore flying in spirit from Friuli to Siberia.

Notes

1. For a more obvious approach see Znamenski 2007:187: "indeed, as student of shamanism, Eliade was a perfect example of an arm-chair scholar – extremely well read in secondary sources, he never observed a single shaman". On Eliade's work, see later.

2. Pike 1967; 1990; Ginzburg 2012b.

3. Ginzburg [1961] 2013a:14.

4. Ginzburg [1988b] 2013e (at that time I was still unaware of Kenneth Pike's dichotomy).

5. Ginzburg 1983:74–77; 1972:11–116.

6. Ginzburg 1993:75–85; 2012b:215–227.

7. Znamenski 2007:184–187. See Eliade 1946; 1951.

8. Znamenski 2007:184–185.

9. Eliade 1975.

10. Ginzburg 2010.

11. de Martino 1948. The manuscript was sent to the publisher, Giulio Einaudi, on August 8, 1946: see Angelini 2007. Translations: English, French, Spanish, Czech, Hungarian, Polish, Japanese.

12. See Ferrari 2012.

13. The blurb refers to de Martino as if had he still been alive (he died in 1964). The first edition, published by Bay Books, Australia, was reprinted by Prism Press in 1988, 1990, 1999. According to a reprint with no date, entitled *The World of Magic*, the English translation was translated from the French version (*Le monde magique*, 1967).

14. Shirokogoroff 1999.

15. de Martino 1999:4 (quoting Shirokogoroff 1935:117ff.) (see de Martino 1948:22–23) I have reinstated the quotation marks in the last sentence.

16. de Martino 1999:5 (quoting Shirokogoroff 1935:117ff.) The passage is omitted (…) in de Martino 1948:23.

17. Znamenski 2007:107–113.

18. Shirokogoroff 1935:42.

19. Shirokogoroff 1924 (this is a revised translation of a paper published in Russian in 1923).

20. Shirokogoroff 1935:23–24.

21. Shirokogoroff 1935:11 note **.

22. Shirokogoroff 1935:360.

23. Shirokogoroff 1935:141.

24. Shirokogoroff 1935:413.

25. Archivio De Martino, 3.8.26 (Charuty 2009:259 note 65; de Martino 1942a. See also de Martino 1942b; de Martino 1943–1946:5: "I principali risultati ottenuti finora (1940)". In 1942, when he received from Father M. Schulien the suggestion to read Shirokogoroff's book, de Martino was already familiar with it (a point missed by Angelini 2008:33–34). Angelini emphasizes (pp. 33–38) the impact of Shirokorogoff's book on de Martino, relying upon the latter's remarks.

26. See de Martino 1948:93 note 2 (misquoted as: *Methode*), 100 note 1. In his first book de Martino had praised Mühlmann's contribution to the *Lehrbuch der Völkerkunde* 1937 as "speculativamente tra i più elevati che ci sia accaduto di leggere nello spoglio che abbiamo fatto della materia": de Martino 1941:197–198 (Mühlmann 1936, is mentioned on p 192 n. 38; see also pp. 193–195). A copy of a later book by Mühlmann 1964, is preserved in de Martino's library (now at the Mediateca dell'Accademia di Santa Cecilia, Roma) with a handwritten dedication: "Dem verherten Kollegen Prof. De Martino zur freundlichen Erinnerung, Roma, 24. April 1965". De Martino died a few days later (May 6).

27. Mühlmann 1936 (*Il mondo*, pp. 94 note 1, 159 note 1). See Reimann & Kiefer (eds.) 1964; 1984; Mühlmann 1968. See Michel 1991; Klingemann 2009:363–373.

28. Mühlmann 1938:158, 162–163 and *passim*. The preface is dated "Hamburg, 13. März 1938. Am Tage der Rückkehr Oesterreichs ins Reich".

29. Mühlmann 1940.

30. See Charuty 2009:254 ff.; Satta 2005.

31. In a conversation which took place in the early '60s in Rome, Angelo Brelich, the historian of religions, remarked that de Martino had tried to grasp "una frangia di ultrastoria". On the intellectual trajectory leading to *Il mondo magico* see my essay Ginzburg 1988a.

32. For a comparison with Adorno and Horkheimer's *Dialectics of the Enlightenment* see Ginzburg 1979b.

33. Charuty 2009:57–59 (quoting passages, translated into French, from de Martino's unpublished notes). A retrospective, not so veiled allusion to this trajectory can be found in de Martino's following remark : "il primitivo, il barbarico, il selvaggio non erano *intorno* a me, perché accadeva talora che anche *dentro* di me sentissi con angoscia risuonare arcaiche voci, e fermentare inclinazioni e suggestioni a comportamenti gratuiti, irrazionali, inquietanti: qualche cosa di caotico e di torbido, che reclamava ordine e luce. Si maturò così un corso di pensieri e di ricerche che mise capo alla tesi fondamentale del *Mondo magico* etc." (de Martino 1953).

34. Ginzburg 1983:XXI (*I benandanti*, p. XIII).

35. Cfr. Klaniczay 2010:203–204.

36. Ginzburg 1981; 1985b (with an introduction by Peter Burke).

37. de Blécourt 2007a:128–129. See also de Blécourt 2007b; 2007c.

38. Ginzburg 1983:28–31.

39. Ginzburg [1985a] 2013d:134.

40. de Blécourt 2007a:128–129.

41. Ginzburg [1979a] 2013b.

42. de Blécourt 2007:139.

43. de Blécourt 2007:139.

44. Ginzburg 1990:203 note 70.

45. Ginzburg 2013f:114.

Shamanism in Classical Scholarship: Where are We Now?

Jan N. Bremmer
University of Groningen, the Netherlands

In memoriam Walter Burkert

There can be no doubt that the idea of shamanism has had a powerful attraction for important and influential classical scholars in the last century. Yet this attention to shamanism was always limited to the small group of classicists that were interested in anthropology and the connections of the classical world with areas beyond the Mediterranean. In my contribution I intend to look again at the most interesting representatives of this interest – Diels, Meuli, Dodds, Burkert – in order to better trace the historiographical development but also note the problems that their proposed solutions raise and the answers that have been given so far. The end result should be a new determination of the *status quaestionis* today.

As I look for the genealogies of the study of ancient shamanism, it might be useful to start with the moment when the shaman first became visible in Western Europe. What is the basis from which the classical scholars started to work? How did the concept of "shaman" find its way into classical scholarship? This problem has been treated by several scholars in the last two decades, but not without some confusion. Fortunately, two recent Groningen dissertations enable us to reach a better picture of the milieu in which Western Europeans became acquainted with the fascinating figure of the shaman.[1] I will start by looking at a trail-blazing article of Carlo Ginzburg (§ 1), then analyse the classical scholars who have connected Greece with shamanism since the end of the 19th-century (§ 2), take a closer look at Aristeas of Proconnesus, one of the showpieces of the thesis of Greek shamanism (§ 3), and conclude with some considerations as to where we are now (§ 4).

How to cite this book chapter:
Bremmer, J. N. 2016. Shamanism in Classical Scholarship: Where are We Now? In: Jackson, P. (ed.) *Horizons of Shamanism: A Triangular Approach to the History and Anthropology of Ecstatic Techniques*. Pp. 52–78. Stockholm: Stockholm University Press. DOI: http://dx.doi.org/10.16993/bag.e. License: CC-BY 4.0

1. The Introduction of the Term "Shaman"[2]

In 1992 Carlo Ginzburg published an erudite article *The Europeans Discover (or Rediscover) the Shamans*, which has deservedly been translated into many languages and has found its definitive form in his recent book *Threads and Traces*. Ginzburg does not mention the place of first publication of his article, but it is not irrelevant to note that these pages first appeared in a kind of *Gedenkschrift* for the already mentioned Karl Meuli (§ 2), which was the result of a conference on Meuli in Basel, his hometown. In his contribution, Ginzburg argued that the first to mention the term "shaman" was the Dutch merchant Evert Ysbrants Ides (1657–1708/09), who registered the existence among the Siberian Tunguses of a "*schaman* or diabolical artist",[3] a word of debated etymology but certainly occurring only among Tunguse-speaking peoples.[4] The son of a Dutch immigrant in the Danish town of Glückstadt, in modern Schleswig-Holstein, Ides had founded a merchant house in Moscow, to which he regularly travelled starting in 1677. Here, in 1691, he met Czar Peter the Great (1672–1725), who, the following year, entrusted him with a mission to the emperor Kangxi of China (1654–1722), with whom he had to initiate commercial contacts and to establish a more precise border between China and Russia after the Peace Treaty of Nerchinsk of 1689.[5]

For his journey, which followed in a zig-zag route the north-south course of the Russian rivers, Ides made use of a map of Siberia which had been made by the Dutch merchant and mayor of Amsterdam Nicolaes Witsen (1641–1717). Probably, Ides had received this map from Witsen's distant cousin and friend Andrej Winius (1641–1717), a member of the circle around the Czar. In 1632, Winius' father had moved to Russia to found a water-powered ironworks in Tula on the Tatar frontier where he married a Russian wife, but he had his sons educated in both Dutch and Russian.[6] Winius was an important source of information regarding Russia for Witsen and had acted as his interpreter during Witsen's visit to Russia in 1664–1665, but the latter carefully omitted the name of his cousin from all his books so that the latter's position at the Russian court would not be compromised.[7] After a trip of 18 months through Siberia and Mongolia Ides and his mission of more than 250 noblemen, advisors, merchants and soldiers reached Bejing in 1693.

Ides' main achievement was that every three years the Russians were allowed to do business in Bejing with a caravan of at most 200 members. However, he did not write his own account of the journey, but gave his papers to the already mentioned Nicolaes Witsen, who finally published the report in 1704 at his own expense.[8] It is not clear why this publication took so long. In 1697 Leibniz was already acquainted with Ides' expedition and mentioned Witsen in this context[9] - an acquaintance less surprising than it might seem at first glance: since 1694 Leibniz and Witsen had been corresponding with each other in French on a wide range of subjects, also on Witsen's *Noord en Oost Tartarije* (below).[10] In any case, Ides' report was a great commercial success, and within a few years it was translated into English, German and French and even, albeit somewhat later, Czech.[11] Strangely, though, Jacobus Scheltema (1767–1835), in his important study of the relations between Russia and the Netherlands, states that the Dutch edition did not appear before 1710,[12] although some copies have 1704 on the title page and the first translations appeared before that date. There seems to be something enigmatic about these early writings on Russia. However this may be, in the book Ides described the Tunguse shaman and provided the first illustration of a shaman in action.[13]

Yet Ides was not the first to mention the term "shaman". As I discovered when studying Ginzburg's article, Ides had been pre-empted by the secretary of his expedition, Adam Brand, a merchant from Lübeck, but perhaps of Dutch origin,[14] who published a brief report of the expedition in 1697 in German.[15] This report proved to be extremely popular in Western Europe, and Leibniz incorporated its contents in his *Novissima Sinica*.[16] The book itself was translated into English in the very same year: *A Journal of an Embassy From Their Majesties John and Peter Alexowits, Emperors of Muscovy, &c, into China, Through the Provinces of Ustiugha, Siberia, Dauri, and the Great Tartary to Peking, the Capital City of the Chinese Empire. Performed by Everard Isbrand, Their Ambassador in the Years 1693, 1694, and 1695. Written by Adam Brand, Secretary of the Embassy* ... (the title is a bibliographer's nightmare), shortly to be followed by Dutch (Tiel, 1699), French (Amsterdam, 1699) and Spanish (Madrid, 1701) translations.[17] The book was also used by Witsen for his edition of Ides' report, as the latter had not always supplied the exact dates in the course of the expedition.[18] Brand mentioned that "where five or six Tunguses live together...they keep a shaman, which means a kind of priest or magician".[19] I concluded, then, that in 1698 Europeans could read the word *shaman* for the very first time.

However, at the very same time that I published my brief study of Greek shamanism, the English historian Ronald Hutton published an attractive book on shamanism and the Western imagination.[20] Given his interest in New Age beliefs and practices, it is not difficult to see why Hutton was interested in the subject, although it may have also helped that he is of Russian ancestry. In his preface he notes that the word "shaman" was "apparently first printed in the (Russian) memoirs" of one of the founders of the so-called Old Believers, Avvakum Petrov (ca. 1620–1682), but "seems to have reached Western and central European scholarship twenty years later in the works of Nicholas Witsen".[21] Regarding Avvakum, this is almost true, as Avvakum indeed uses a form of the verb "to shamanize" (*shamanit*), although not the noun "shaman".[22] Regarding the latter, Hutton is still somewhat doubtful, as he writes "seems to have reached".

However, all doubts have disappeared in Kocku von Stuckrad's study on shamanism and esotericism, which appeared shortly after Hutton's book and my own; in fact, having been a member of his Habilitation committee I alerted him to both studies, which he had not yet seen at the time. Von Stuckrad notes: "Jan Bremmer (…) bezeichnet Brand 1698 als die erste literarische Erwähnung des Begriffs (of the shaman); dieses Privileg kommt jedoch tatsächlich Witsen 1692 (1705) zu".[23] Evidently, Von Stuckrad took his cue from Hutton but, like Hutton, he overlooked an important aspect of Witsen's book.

Witsen published the first edition of his famous book *Noord en Oost Tartarije* in Amsterdam in 1692.[24] Its circulation must have been very low, as there are only four copies surviving, two in St. Petersburg, one in Utrecht and one in Amsterdam.[25] The reasons for this scarcity remain obscure but the fortune of his second edition was not that much better. Although the title page carries the year 1705, the first copies of the second edition appeared on the market only in 1747, thirty years after Witsen's death, once again for reasons that have not yet been clarified.[26] But whatever the reasons, for us it is much more important to note that there are significant differences. The second edition was wholly remade and expanded on the basis of additional and up-to-date information, such as the report of the expedition of Ides. Moreover, the plates in Witsen's second edition are often the same as those in Ides' book, and seem to derive from the same designer and printer who, unfortunately, have not yet been identified.[27] Von Stuckrad, who clearly did not make the effort to compare the two editions, thus missed the differences between them and wrongly credited Witsen with the first mention.[28]

At the same time, we should note that the emergence of the term "shaman" has to be located in a specific network in Amsterdam around 1700 with Nicolaes Witsen as the spider in the web. It was his personal network and commercial interests that had promoted the production of Russian maps and reports of journeys in Russia. The discovery of the "shaman" was a fortunate by-product of this interest, but the figure was strange enough to become soon a focus of interest in the European Republic of Letters.[29]

2. Rohde, Diels, Meuli, Dodds, Burkert[30]

After Brand, Ides and Witsen, it would take some time before shamans entered the classical world. The first to compare Greek figures to shamans was probably Herder (1744–1803), who in a 1777 essay about the similarity of the older English and German poetry wrote that Arion, Orpheus and Amphion would have been "edle griechische Schamanen" when they lived.[31] This is still how the Romantic Movement pictures shamanism, but we come closer to modern views in that masterpiece *Aglaophamus* of the very learned but also very critical Christian August Lobeck (1781–1860), who in a note in his book argued that, if we wanted to, we could call Epimenides a priest, just like the Pythagorean Apollonius of Tyana and, as he notes in a surprising comparison, *hodie sunt Schamani*. Lobeck even adds that *re vera* they were just as much priests as *Empedocles aut Abaris aut Pythagoras*.[32] Unfortunately, Lobeck does not enlarge upon his comments or add references to literature regarding the shamans, but it is interesting for us to see that he already groups together several figures from the Archaic and earlier Classical period who we will also meet as a shamanic group in later writings.

Interestingly, there are two more unnoticed references to ancient shamanism in German classical scholarship that suggest that there was perhaps more attention to shamanism in connection with ancient Greece than we nowadays are inclined to suppose. In a mid-19th-century commentary on Herodotus, we find the shamans quoted in notes on Herodotus' description of divination practices of the Scythians.[33] The source of the commentary in this respect was the study of the ancient historian and geographer Karl Neumann (1823–1880), who had written his dissertation about Crimean Olbia. In a study of the Greeks in the land of the Scythians, the learned Neumann compares in detail some of Herodotus' information regarding Scythian divination and sacrifice, as well as the report that their women have two pupils in their eyes, with that of shamanistic practices of the Mongols, Buryats and other Siberian tribes.[34] Not surprisingly, we will meet his name regularly in the notes of Meuli's study on Scythian shamanism (below).

Although the nexus Greeks-Scythians-shamans has roots going back to the middle of the 19th-century, Wilhelm Radloff's 1884 *Aus Siberien* was probably the work most influential in animating interest in shamanism among leading classicists of the late 19th-century. Radloff (1837–1918) gave a fascinating description of a shamanic séance, a real "thick description", which still impresses by its attention to detail and liveliness. Yet Radloff was honest enough to stress that it is very difficult to give a precise definition of shamanism, as all tribes had variants of its beliefs and practices; moreover, because of the absence of written sources we have little idea of their history and authoritative traditions. Shamanism was of course less worthy than the three great religions of Christianity, Islam and Buddhism but it had its own value, and the shamans were not really less respectable than many Christian, i.e. Roman-Catholic, priests, according to Radloff.[35]

Radloff's description of the shaman is rightly called an "unvergleichlich anschaulige Darstellung" by Erwin Rohde (1845–1898). In his masterpiece *Psyche*, Rohde does not really use shamanism as a comparative element in order to explain Greek phenomena, but he sees shamans as one manifestation of the masters of ecstasy who through their exhausting dances effect a "besonders energischer Glaube an Leben und Kraft der vom Leibe getrennten Seele des Menschen". In the end, it is this ecstasy, which is not exclusively shamanic, that Rohde sees at the basis of man's belief in the immortality of the soul. Rohde also adduced shamans to explain the lack of pain the maenads feel in Euripides' *Bacchae*, but again in this case the shamans are just one category among yogis, dervishes and the native North Americans.[36] Unlike Von Stuckrad,[37] we should therefore be reticent in attributing an all too great influence on later theories to him, even though Rohde had already collected virtually all the figures that Meuli, Dodds and Burkert would interpret as shamanic.[38]

The second eminent classicist who adduced parallels from shamanism was Rohde's contemporary Hermann Diels (1848–1922). In an 1897 article, he noted similarities between Anaximander's construction of the cosmos and that of shamanistic Mongolian tribes, but he also referred to the *Kalevala*, one of the shamanic texts which Meuli (below) was interested in. In his book *Parmenides*, which appeared in the very same year, he used Radloff's, as he called it, "klassische Schilderung", as the basis for his knowledge of shamanism although his interest went further than that. In rather Christianizing terminology ("Apostel", "Kirche", "Reformation", "Propheten", "Sündenfall" and "Sündenvergebung"), Diels grouped together a series of, as he called them, "Wundermänner", who indeed become visible in our evidence at the end of the Archaic period, around 500 BC. As with Lobeck, we find here, Abaris, Pythagoras and the Cretan diviner and purifier Epimenides, but also Parmenides himself, Empedocles, a certain Aithalides who had received the gift from Hermes that his soul could stay in the underworld and in the area above earth (*Pherecydes* B 8 DK), a Syracusan called Empedotimos of whom an ascent to heaven was told, the military commander Phormio about whom a visionary journey from Sparta to Croton, the hometown of Pythagoras, was related, and Aristeas, to whom we will return shortly (§ 3). In other words, in Diels we find the "usual suspects" of all those that are currently connected to shamanism.

However, it should be stressed that Diels did not accept shamanistic influence on ancient Greece. He saw the similarities more
on a phenomenological than a genealogical level,[39] an attitude that
was in line with that of Wilamowitz (1848–1931), the greatest
classicist of that era, if not of all time, who was averse to any outside influence on his beloved Greeks.[40] That is perhaps why Diels
had less influence than the two scholars who really put ancient
shamanism on the map, Meuli and Dodds, to whom we turn now.

Meuli (1891–1968) was both a professor extraordinarius at the
University of Basel (and from 1942 an ordinarius) in Classics and
Folklore as well as a teacher of Classics at the local Humanisti-
sches Gymnasium.[41] His learned oeuvre stands at the crossroads
of classics, folklore, ethnology, psychology and the history of religion, and still impresses by its mastery of the sources and its careful, elegant style of writing. Unfortunately, we do not know how
exactly Meuli came to shamanism. In my 2002 book I was still
inclined to ascribe the main influence in this respect to Rohde, as
Meuli had followed lectures in Munich in 1911–12, amongst others, with Rohde's biographer Otto Crusius (1857–1918), whom he
highly respected.[42] Yet the absence in Rohde of any detailed reference to specific Greek shamans, makes me now realise that Meuli
must have been especially inspired by Diels' *Parmenides*, whose
study of Parmenides he calls a "meisterhafte Untersuchung", and
whose characterization of Radloff's description as the "klassische
Schilderung" he explicitly quotes.[43]

Meuli's interest in shamanism becomes visible first in a passage
from an article from 1924 on the bath of the Scythians, but it
came to full fruition only in 1935 in his classic article *Scythica*, in
which he concentrated on three aspects: 1. the Scythian shamans
in Herodotus; 2. the transvestite Scythian seers; 3. the shaman
and his poetry.[44] When we now read the article with critical eyes
and do not let ourselves be swept away by its beautiful style and
persuasive rhetoric, we can only conclude that in all three cases
Meuli could only succeed in proving the existence of Scythian shamanism and the influence of that shamanism via several examples
of sleights of hand.

In his discussion of Herodotus' description of the Scythians'
funeral customs, Meuli focuses on the howling of the Scythians

in their vapor bath with hemp. Quoting a description by Radloff of a shamanic purification of a yurt, Meuli interprets the howling as the singing of the shaman in order to guide the soul of the deceased to the beyond. Now Meuli was too honest a scholar not to observe that in Herodotus' description all classic characteristics of shamanism are lacking: there is no mention of spirits, no mention of a drum, an indispensable part of Siberian shamanism,[45] and, above all, there is no mention of a shaman! Meuli therefore suggested that the Scythians did not yet have professional shamans but knew an older stage of shamanism, family shamanism ("Familien-Schamanismus"), which could still be observed among modern day Siberian peoples, such as the Goldi, Votyak and Ostyak, or, as they are called today, the Nanai (or Nanay), the Urmurt and the Khanti (or Khanty). Yet among all these tribes hereditary shamanism is well attested.[46] When we now also take into account that Meuli himself notes that the ritual is described by Herodotus with great accuracy,[47] one cannot but conclude that he failed to substantiate his thesis at this point.

As regards his second point, Meuli focuses on the Enarees, of whom Herodotus (1.105, 4.67.2) relates that they were a Scythian group of seers who were the descendants of those Scythians that had plundered the temple of Aphrodite in Ascalon and were punished by the goddess with the "female disease", that is, made impotent. Consequently, as we hear from the author of a Hippocratic treatise (Aer. 22), they dressed in female clothes and performed female tasks, such as weaving, which looks like a Greek elaboration of the "female disease".[48] The Hippocratic author calls them Anarieis, which comes closer than Enarees to the undoubtedly Iranian origin of the name, which should not be explained, as Meuli does, from Iranian *a-nar, "not having a man", but from a-narya:h, "not masculine". The variation Anarieis/ Enarees, with the typical Greek a>e adaptation of Iranian names, probably suggests that the Greeks learned of these seers along different routes.[49] Not surprisingly, Meuli compares them with reports of Siberian males who acted as shamans in female clothes, although not always without having sexual relations with women. Although Meuli himself notes that the closest parallels occur among the most eastern Siberian tribes,[50] this does not prevent him from declaring that "Die existenz eines echtskythischen Schamanismus ist damit bewiesen". Moreover, by combining the two Herodotean passages about the funeral and the Enarees, Meuli first promotes all the howling Scythians to being shamans and then also promotes the Enarees to a shamanic status, whereas Herodotus describes them only as effeminate seers belonging to the elite.[51] However, despite his claim that apparently all Scythians were shamans, Meuli must have felt a bit uncertain about the lack of shamanism in what we know about the ancient Iranian religion.[52] This led him to deduce the journeys of the Mithraic initiates into the otherworld as closely related to those of the "primitiven Schamanen", a most unlikely suggestion.[53] I conclude, therefore, that at this point, also, Meuli has not proven the existence of Scythian shamanism.[54]

His final point concerns shamanism and Greek poetry. After an interesting account of shamanistic poetry, Meuli first discusses Aristeas and Abaris, figures already identified as shamanoid by Lobeck and Diels, as we saw.[55] I will come back to Aristeas shortly (§ 3), but note that Meuli promoted both of them to the status of "skythischer Wundermann", although there is no evidence at all in our sources that they were Scythians.[56] The only other figure Meuli considers as shamanic is Zalmoxis, a Thracian whom the Greeks associated with Pythagoras in a manner that has not yet been satisfactorily explained and will not occupy us here.[57] Having looked at these figures, Meuli concluded: "Die Existenz einer skythischen Schamanendichtung, die bei so entwickeltem Schamanentum ohnehin anzunehmen war, darf nun als erwiesen gelten". This is of course a rhetorical trick, as Meuli had proved neither the existence of Scythian shamans nor the existence of Scythian shamanic poetry. But he needed this conclusion in order to reach the point he wanted to make, that is, that the journeys of Odysseus and the Argonauts in Greek epic went back to shamanistic poetry. Needless to say, a sober look at the evidence does not provide any proof of these suggestions despite all Meuli's erudition.

After a brief comparison of Greek heroic poetry with the *Kalevala*, which had already been adduced by Diels, Meuli ended with:

"Es ist wahrlich nichts geringes, dass die finnischen Sänger dank Umständen, die hier nicht zu untersuchen sind, uns einen Schatz von liedern bewahrt haben, die, ihrem Wesen nach weit älter als

Homer, zu den ältesten und ehrwürdigsten Formen der Poesie gezählt werden müssen".

Von Stuckrad quotes this conclusion, too, and remarks: "Diese Darstellung ist der germanischen Rhetorik der 'Herrenrasse' ebenso verpflichtet wie den Konstruktionen des edlen griechischen 'Geschlechtes', die sich dem 19. Jahrhundert verdanken".[58] Nothing could be further from the truth. Meuli had nothing to do with the contemporary Nazi ideology, and his whole oeuvre testifies to a view of Greece that does not stress its superiority but its indebtedness to Central Asiatic traditions. In 1940, in support of the Finnish war effort against the Russians, Meuli returned to the problem of shamanism in a brief piece on the *Kalevala*, in which he postulated shamanic poetry as its core, and in a lecture given in 1950, but which was only published in 1975, he postulated Orpheus as an "Urbild eines Schamanen". He remained interested in shamanism until the end of his life,[59] but his work became really influential only through the use made of it by Dodds.

Unlike Meuli, Eric Robertson Dodds, Regius Professor of Greek at Oxford, (1893–1979),[60] invested most of his scholarly time in books, three of which – his commentary on Euripides' *Bacchae* (1944), *The Greeks and the Irrational* (1951), and *Pagan and Christian in an Age of Anxiety* (1965) – are still being reprinted and translated, thus making him the most influential English classicist of the 20th-century in international terms. Yet it is especially his book about the Greeks and the irrational that has been the most influential. This is also the book that popularized the notion of the shaman well into the twenty-first century. However, Dodds' use of the idea of shamanic influence was completely different from that of Meuli, as he wanted to explain the rise of the notion of the immortal soul in Greece, which he saw as something new and alien to Greek culture. That is why he latched on to the idea of shamanistic influence. Dodds thus accepted Diels' and Meuli's arguments without any criticism, and even expanded Meuli's collection of shamanic figures by incorporating Pythagoras, Empedocles and, without knowing Meuli's posthumously published study, Orpheus, whom he interpreted as "a mythical shaman or prototype of shamans".[61]

It is rather odd that Dodds explains the growth of a certain Puritanism, which he perceives in Archaic and early Classical

Greece, as the result of the impact of shamanistic beliefs. The little that we know about Scythia and Thrace gives no information at all about shamanistic beliefs. It is clear that, basically, Dodds was at a loss as how to elucidate the rise of the independent soul, a problem that has indeed not yet been satisfactorily explained.[62] Apparently, there are too few data to lead us towards a specific explanatory path and the available traditions can be juggled into several directions without our evidence giving us sufficient guidance.

It is noteworthy that Walter Burkert (1931–2015) realised this problem to a certain extent. He had got to know Meuli through Reinhold Merkelbach (1918–2006), who was well to do and had been able to restore contacts with Switzerland fairly early after the war. Merkelbach, then professor of Greek in Erlangen where Burkert was *Assistent* at the time, was an admirer of Meuli, and one of the driving forces behind the publication of the latter's *Gesammelte Schriften*. Burkert shares this admiration, as also appears from his famous book on sacrifice, *Homo Necans* (1972). It is therefore not surprising that Burkert was inspired by Meuli's study of shamanism, although he of course also admired Dodds and Diels, whose *Kleine Schriften* he edited. Following Diels, Dodds and Meuli in his *Habilitationsschrift* (1962) about Pythagoras, Burkert not only put Pythagoras and the now "usual suspects", such as Aristeas and Abaris, in a shamanistic framework but he also discussed the problem of Greek shamanism in a separate article, which has received less attention than it deserves.[63]

In this article Burkert starts by wondering whether the adduced shamanic motifs, such as journeys to the Beyond, are simply "legendäre Wandermotive" or practiced rituals, either as survivals from time immemorial or revivals due to foreign influence. He does not answer the question but directs his attention to a word that he considers to have a noteworthy "Affinität zum Schamanenbereich", namely γόης, which he translates with the Scottish classicist John Burnet (1863–1928) as "Medizinmann". He then continues by arguing that the γόης was the closest equivalent to the Siberian shaman. But is that really true?

Burkert starts with the reference in the archaic epic *Phoronis* (fr. 2 Bernabé) to the Idaean Dactyls, smiths who were also γόητες, "sorcerers", and who engaged in "incantations, initiations and mysteries". Apparently, the combination with incantations is very important, as a number of passages in Greek literature combine these with sorcerers or sorcery.[64] Burkert sees the bridge between these two in *Musikmagie* and subsequently extrapolates from the calling up of Persephone in Eleusis with a gong and the fact that necromancers are connected with "sorcering" a close connection between the "sorcerer" and the cult of the dead. He also notes the report by Herodotus that each year the Scythian Neuroi morphed into wolves for a few days and naturally concludes that these people must be "sorcerers". Yet the fact that Herodotus locates these Neuroi next to the cannibalistic Androphagi suggests a certain fictional content in this report.[65] However, Burkert concludes from his examples that there were certain persons in olden times who were the centre of ritual and cult: "Medizinmänner, Schamanen, Zauberpriester".[66]

Burkert proceeds with the etymology of γόης and concludes from the use of the corresponding verb γοάω and related adjectives that its basic meaning was "to lament". Consequently, he argues, the γόης was "the wailer", the performer of the funeral lament. Unfortunately, one must object: there is not a single passage in Greek literature where the term has the postulated meaning. Moreover, Burkert has also to resort to some hermeneutical juggling as he notes the absence of an ecstatic *Jenseitsreise* in the case of the γόης, despite the fact that such a journey to the Beyond "ein besonderes Charakteristicum des Schamanen ist", but suggests that the "oft hervorgehobene Kunst der Verwandlung in gewissem Masse äquivalent ist" – which is not immediately persuasive. One can therefore only agree with him that "Ein direkter Beleg für entwickelte Schamanenpraxis ist allerdings in unserer Überlieferung nicht zu finden",[67] and neither is an indirect one, I may add.

Moreover, it is not true that the negative meaning of γόης is a gradual development. From the very beginning, we can note a combination of the γόης with magic and incantations. It seems that the term, which etymologically means "the shouter",[68] developed in two directions. On the one hand, among women it became used for wailing and lamenting, whereas among men it seems to have been used for the loud performing of incantations. At least that is the most natural explanation, given its frequent combination with incantations (above) from the very beginning. In any case, the term always has a negative meaning and is never a self-designation. To postulate it as "zum Schimpfwort abgesunken" lacks any basis in our evidence.[69] I can only conclude that this attempt at introducing the shamanic model as a major hermeneutical tool for Greek religion has not been successful.

Burkert returned to shamanism in 1972 in the English version of his *Weisheit und Wissenschaft*. In the preface he notes that "more thorough acquaintance with ancient religion has pushed the concept of "shamanism" further into the background", and in his classic handbook of Greek religion, originally published in 1977, shamanism makes only a fleeting appearance.[70] Yet in his 1979 study on the Master of Animals he took up the theme again, but introduced a new twist. Now he explained Heracles' hunting of the herd of Geryon from a primeval shamanistic motif that can still be witnessed among Arctic and Siberian peoples in the recent past, and with roots going back to "the darkness of prehistory".[71] No more Scythians here! Shamanism has now become one of the strata of man's civilization of which certain strands survived into the historical period. It is not surprising, then, that in the "Addendum 2003" to the reprint of his 1962 article Burkert rejects my plea for "a more detailed definition of the shamanistic complex", and pleads for "shamanism" (his inverted commas!) as a way to explain *Jenseitsreisen* in connection with certain ritual practices.[72]

3. Aristeas of Proconnesus

In his *Ecstasies* Carlo Ginzburg basically follows Meuli and looks for a historical connection between Greece and the Scythians to explain the shamanistic motifs in early Greek culture. He does not survey all figures traditionally connected to Greek shamanism, but just mentions Aristeas of Proconnesus. As he is also the only shamanic figure that has received special attention in the last decade, it may be worthwhile to have a second look at him in order to get the problem of Greek shamanism into better focus.[73] Let us not rehearse here the whole of his story but just the beginning as related by Herodotus:

> "Aristeas also, the son of Kaystrobios, a native of Proconnesus, says in the course of his poem that, possessed by Apollo, he reached the Issedonians. Above them dwelt the Arimaspi, men with one eye; still further, the gold-guarding griffins, and beyond these, the Hyperboreans, whose country extended to the sea. Except the Hyperboreans, all these nations, beginning with the Arimaspi, continually encroached on their neighbours. Hence it came to pass that the Arimaspi gradually drove the Issedonians from their country, while the Issedonians dispossessed the Scyths; and the Scyths, pressing upon the Cimmerians, who dwelt on the shores of the southern sea, forced them to leave their land" (4.13, tr. Bolton).

I have limited my quotation for the moment to these lines, as they are sufficient to establish certain data about Aristeas. The name of his father Kaystrobios means "gift of Kaystros", and the first part, Kaystro-, often occurs in Ionian names.[74] This firmly establishes his father as an Ionian who, presumably, had emigrated to Proconnesus, an island in the Sea of Marmara. His son Aristeas was the author of a poem. As we have a number of lines of that poem, the *Arimaspea*, the safest way of dating Aristeas is through an analysis of the words of his poem and their chronological occurrence in Greek poetry. Such an analysis was first carried out by Bolton in an excellent book on Aristeas and his analysis has subsequently been refined by Ivantchik. The latter reaches the conclusion that the language of the poem dates from about 500 BC, which comes close to Jacoby's placement of the poem in the second half of the sixth century BC.[75] The date is confirmed by the iconography of Greek vases where the battle between the Arimaspi and the griffins, which is described later by Herodotus, starts to appear around 515 BC;[76] the oldest reference to the poem, by Pindar (F 271 Maehler), fits this date also. Consequently, the poet must have lived in the second half of the sixth century BC. His Ionian father may well have still heard oral tales about the fall of Sardis to the Cimmerians and their expulsion by the Scythians from Asia Minor in the middle of the seventh century – given the mention of Cimmerians and Scythians in Aristeas' poem.

The relatively late date makes it much more likely that Aristeas heard stories from the Scythian areas than the traditional seventh-century date would have allowed, as it is hard to think of a Greek traveling in Scythia in the seventh century.[77] Without a "Rough Guide", how would he have found his way in a land without landmarks and with inhabitants whose languages he did not speak? It is one thing to hear of stories about gold-guarding ants, but a rather different matter to become trained as a shaman and to be able to go into trance with a concept of the soul foreign to one's habitus.[78] Given that Herodotus certainly wrote about a century after Aristeas we should also wonder about the historical value of the traditions he recorded in Proconnesus, as these look very much like later embellishments. This is even truer for what he heard in Metapontum. Here, as Herodotus was told, Aristeas re-appears 240 years after his disappearance in Proconnesus and told the Metapontines that he followed Apollo in the shape of a raven. We need not go as far as Bolton and speculate that Pythagoras himself was especially interested in the *Arimaspea*,[79] but the re-appearance after death, the closeness to Apollo (the main god of Metapontum) and the metamorphosis into a raven, Apollo's bird, clearly all point to a Pythagorean background with Metapontum as centre. It is not surprising, then, that in the catalogue of the Pythagoreans reported by Iamblichus, which goes back to the fourth-century BC Aristoxenus, we find an Aristeas among the Pythagoreans of Metapontum.[80] In the end there is no early shamanistic detail left of Aristeas' legends that is credibly derived from the Scythians.[81]

4. Where are we now?

It is perhaps not surprising that after the expansive views of Greek shamanism a reaction set in, first by myself and directed especially against the expositions of Meuli and Dodds, then by Fritz Graf against the shamanistic interpretation of Orpheus and, last but not least, by the late Pierre Hadot (1922–2010) and the Russian scholar Leonid Zhmud against Burkert's shamanising interpretation of Pythagoras.[82] Altogether these investigations have gradually dismantled the edifice built by Meuli, Dodds and Burkert and shown that none of the proposed derivations from the Scythians holds up or even that the Scythians themselves had a shamanistic religion. At the same time we could not but note that the shamanistic concept served very different purposes: for Meuli it explained the origins of epic poetry, for Dodds the origin of the immortal soul and the rise of charismatics such as Empedocles, and for Burkert the legends surrounding Pythagoras. In other words, shamanism was, so to speak, a joker that could be put on the table to explain developments for which scholars were unable to produce an internal Greek explanation.[83]

Now where classical critics focused on the "diffusionist" approach, Von Stuckrad has approached the problem from a different angle.[84] He rightly argues that when scholars adduce modern descriptions of shamanism to explain ancient phenomena, they inevitably presuppose the unchanging character of shamanistic cultures, whereas everything we know suggests that these did not stand outside the flow of history. This is certainly true, although we also should observe that at the time of the supposed shamanistic influence on Greece, that is around 500 BC, Central Asia had not yet experienced the shock waves of Buddhism, Islam or Christianity.

On the other hand, it seems less helpful to speak, as von Stuckrad proposes, of a *schamanistische Matrix*, which consists of "Transformation, Jenseitsreise, Initiation, Heilung, Kommunikation mit Toten, Trennung von Körper und Seele sowie aussergewöhnliche Bewusstseinszustände, die in der Regel durch Musik induziert werden".[85] Von Stuckrad clearly fails to realise that he has arrived at his *Matrix* from the very modern descriptions he first considered unusable to interpret ancient phenomena.[86] Moreover, he pleads to use only emic concepts, which is never helpful,[87] and succumbs to the magic of the γόης by considering that figure a helpful tool for a better understanding of the "shamanistic" figures without noting that it is a term of abuse, not a self-designation, and that there never was a recognizable figure in Greece that matched his *Matrix*.

A rather different direction was taken by the great French scholar Louis Gernet (1882–1962), a member of the Durkheim school, in a generally neglected article of 1945. He looked at the same "shamanoid" figures as Diels and Meuli had investigated, but tried to illuminate the various traditions from the pre-history of the Greeks, even extending his explanatory framework to the Indo-Europeans. Thus Gernet explained the connection of Pythagoras with the divine from Frazer's magical king of the *Golden Bough*. Gernet's contribution is without notes, but the brief remark that the notion of the soul that has been picked up by Platonism was once associated with "quelque chose comme une discipline de *shaman*" leaves little doubt that Gernet also knew Meuli's article. However, Gernet realized that he spoke more of "antécédents plûtot qu'un passage".[88] One need not follow Gernet in his Frazerian approach, but it is indeed a fact that the mythical figure of Orpheus and the activities of the Cretan Epimenides (firmly dated to about 600 BC) suggest that the roots of these figures go back into times that are no longer accessible for historical research.

Unlike Gernet, his pupil Jean-Pierre Vernant (1914–2007) was the first to attack this problem in a 1959 article, entitled "From Myth to Reason", in which he tried to explain the "shamanoid" figures without taking recourse to the shamanic paradigm, although even he could not wholly escape the fascination of the shaman. Vernant notes the high social status of the first philosophers, coming from priestly families, who now put their priestly secrets in the open air. More importantly, he connects the transition from the Archaic Age to the classical era with the combined birth of the polis, the growth of politics, the rise of mathematics, and the emergence of money.[89] Although seemingly without knowledge of Vernant's article, Burkert refined this line of thought in his γόης study. He persuasively argues that the polis no longer had room for the exceptional individual, and, as I have argued, it is this reduction of possibilities for the nobility to stand out in this life that promoted a belief in reincarnation, which would still guarantee them a special status, even if perhaps only in the life hereafter.[90] Yet, in contrast to Gernet's observation, these arguments may explain their disappearance, but they do not illuminate the antecedents of the "shamanoid" figures.

So where are we now after the dismantling of the shamanic paradigm? We have seen how the best Hellenists of the last century have wrestled with the problem of the appearance in our sources of people who were reputed to be able to go into a trance and to fly, to practice a special life style or to possess extraordinary knowledge. Their interest in this theme could make them members of a *Faszinationsgemeinschaft* as defined by Martin Mulsow:[91] whatever their solution, all these scholars were clearly fascinated by the charismatic outsiders, who are so different from the rational Greeks as we like to see them, and their fascination led them to sometimes uncritical acceptance of the shamanistic theses. Yet their studies also have greatly elucidated the various traditions of the "shamanic" figures and their mutual relationships".[92]

This conclusion does not preclude the possibility of cultural and religious transfers between Central/South East Asia and Greek culture, not even an influence from shamanistic cultures. Aristeas' poem told of journeys to fabulous peoples and of gold-guarding griffins fighting with the one-eyed Arimaspi, a passage that surely is a double of Herodotus' report about gold-guarding ants in the Bactrian desert. The story is well attested in ancient Indian sources and probably derives from Dardistan where the burrowing of marmots in the gold-bearing soil was regularly exploited.[93] In his recent book on Indo-European myth and poetry, Martin West has suggested that the Greeks and Indians derived their ideas of reincarnation from a common source somewhere in the Persian Empire. Yet if we take into account that the Buddha has been down-dated in recent decades, the chance is not imaginary that the Indians were, directly or indirectly, influenced by the Greeks in this respect.[94] West also compares the close parallels between the role of the raven in the myths of Germanic Odin, Celtic Lug and Greek Apollo and ascribes them to the influence of Finno-Ugric peoples in different directions. Perhaps this is possible, but one must also observe that Odin and Lug have two ravens, Apollo just one. In fact, Apollo really appears too late in Greek religion to be persuasively compared with Odin and Lug, the more so as he probably derives from pre-Indo-European Western Anatolia.[95] The existence of a kind of world pillar, on the other hand, looks specific enough to be derived from Central Asiatic cosmology, but we do not know when that happened.[96] In the end, though, it is easier to accept that the Greeks derived some mythological details from Central Asia than that they imported complex ritual practices that presuppose a new concept of the soul.

In reaction to the shamanistic approach, Gernet, as we saw, attempted to situate the "shamanoid" figures in the heritage of the Greeks from their religious prehistory, even if with many permutations in the course of time. On the other hand, more recent scholarship has not looked into the Greek hoary past but has concentrated on internal developments at the time of the transition of the Archaic to the classical age. It seems to me that future research should try to combine all three approaches. There can be little doubt that the Greek "shamans" did not appear from nowhere but made use of practices and ideas that had "une très longue histoire", to quote Gernet one last time.[97] At the same time we need not exclude the possibility of religious transfers from the Thracians or Scythians, but we should be more rigorous in our explanations than Meuli and his followers have been. Finally, we should try to trace the political, cultural, economic and religious developments that created the world in which these figures could operate but from which they also disappeared. This is not an easy task, and we must somewhat sadly conclude that, despite all the efforts of the best classical scholars of the last century, we can still see these Greek "shamans" only through a glass darkly.[98]

Abbreviations

DK : Diels/Kranz, *Die Fragmente der Vorsokratiker*
ad FGrH : *addenda, Fragmente der griechischen Historiker*
LIMC : *Lexicon Iconographica Mythologiae Classicae*
VP : *De Vita Pythagorica*
NH : *Naturalis Historia*

Notes

1. Wladimiroff 2008; Peters 2008, revised and well illustrated as Peters 2010.

2. In this section I correct, update and expand my earlier discussion in Bremmer 2002a:27–28.

3. Ginzburg 1992:121, reprinted (corrected and updated) in Ginzburg 2012a:82–95, 260–66 (notes).

4. For the most recent discussion, see Knüppel 2010.

5. For Ides, see Treichel 1976; Wladimiroff 2008:171–74.

6. Seymour 1855:73; Baron 1967:124 n. 32.

7. Peters 2008:81–84; 2010:103–12; Wladimiroff 2008.

8. Scheltema 1817–1819:2.93.

9. See the letter to the Orientalist W.H. Ludolf (1624–1704) by Leibniz 1993:555 (d.d. 2/10 October 1697).

10. Müller 1955:20–22.

11. Cf. Tiele 1966:118; van Eeghen 1978:103–104; Tavernier 2006:nos 768–80.

12. Scheltema 1817–1819:2.93.

13. *Driejaarige reize naar China te lande gedaan door den Moskovischen Afgezant, E. Ysbrants Ides, van Moskou af, over Groot Ustiga, Siriania, Permia, Siberien, Daour, Groot Tartaryen tot in China ...* (Amsterdam, 1704, repr. 1710) 34–35.

14. Thus Scheltema 1817–1819:2.92, who calls him a Dutch merchant.

15. Brand(t) 1698, reprinted in Hundt 1999:109–89, where also a good discussion of the immediate reception of the work (p. 68–70).

16. Leibniz 1697; cf. Leibniz, edited and translated by Nesselrath and Reinbothe 1979, reprinted with bibliographical updates by Paul and Grünert 2010.

17. Cf. Kazanin (ed.) 1967:365–77 (add the Spanish translation); Hund 1999:68.

18. Peters 2008:91; 2010:120.

19. Brand 1698:80–81; Hund 1999:141: "Wo fünf oder sechs Tungusen bey einander wohnen...halten sie einen Schaman, welcher auf ihre Art einen Pfaffen oder Zauberer bedeutet".

20. Hutton 2001.

21. Hutton 2001:vii, elaborated at p. 32, where he quotes the third edition of 1785, for which see Peters 2008:143–144; 2010:196–197. However, Avvakum's book was printed only in 1861.

22. Cf. Rzhevsky 1996:566 n. 63. As Leonid Zhmud points out to me (email 3-4-2015), Avvakum's book "contains also a toponym Шаманской порог (*Shamanskoi porog*, *porog* = rapids) on the river Tunguska. To the shaman himself he applies an old Russian word волхв, i.e. a pagan soothsayer, sorcerer".

23. von Stuckrad 2003:43 n. 34, 44 n. 36.

24. For the precise meaning of Tartarije in those days, see Köhler 2012:61–62.

25. Peters 2008:134–40; 2010:184–93.

26. Peters 2008:140–43; 2010:193–96.

27. Peters 2008:149–151; 2010:208–14.

28. Similarly, Znamenski 2007:5, 372 note 8, who mistakenly thinks that the edition of 1785 is just a reprint of that of 1692. von Stuckrad returned to the subject in von Stuckrad 2012:100–121, repeating his statement that "shaman" can be found first in Witsen, but now without any mention of Ginzburg and Bremmer.

29. Flaherty 1992; Boekhoven 2011:32–38.

30. In this section I summarize, correct and expand Bremmer 2002:28–36.

31. Herder 1807:65.

32. Lobeck 1829:13–14, note h.

33. Bähr et al. 1857:435 on Hdt 4.67 where Bähr sometimes offers more interesting material than the recent commentary of Corcella ad loc.

34. Neumann 1852; 1855:247, 250, 265–68. On Neumann, see Kupferschmidt 1935.

35. Radloff 1884:2.1–67. On Radloff, see Temir 1955; Harvilahti 2000; Znamenski 2007:33–38.

36. Rohde 1898:2.18 note 3 (maenads), 24–33 (ecstasy and the soul). Note that these shamans do not yet appear in the first edition of *Psyche* (1894), but were clearly added after Diels' 1897 article (below).

37. von Stuckrad 2003:98.

38. Rohde 1898:2.90–102.

39. Diels 1897:14–21 (the various shamans); 1969:18–20 (1897[1]: *Kalevala* and Anaximander); at the end of his life 1922:239–240.

40. For Wilamowitz and Greek religion, see Henrichs 1985; Fowler 2009; Bremmer 2010a:7–10.

41. For biographies of Meuli, see Jung 1975; Bonjour 1994; Baumgarten 2012; see also the illuminating studies of Meuli's work in Graf 1992.

42. For Meuli in Munich, see Meuli 1975:2.735 (respect for Crusius), 1158–1160 (Munich), 1172 (Rohde's *Psyche*); Henrichs 1992:159–160. For Crusius, see Pfeiffer 1957:432 (with further bibliography).

43. Thus, rightly, Jung 1975:2.1200 note 1, cf. Meuli 1975:2.820 ("klassische Schilderung"), 858–859 (Diels' *Parmenides*), 873 ("meisterhafte Untersuchung").

44. Meuli 1935; 1975:2.817–873.

45. Hultkrantz 1991.

46. Meuli 1975:2.822, cf. Eliade 1964:15 (Votyak, Ostyak); Delaby 1977:33 (Goldi); note also the objections of Dowden 1980:486–487. For Eliade's classic study, see now Casadio 2014.

47. Meuli 1975:2.822–823.

48. Lieber 1996.

49. *Contra* Meuli 1975:2.828. I am most grateful to Norbert Oettinger (Erlangen) for an enlightening discussion of this problem (email 1-11-2013).

50. Meuli 1975:2.826; similarly, Eliade 1964:258; for a possible exception, see Basilov 1978; in general, Bleibtreu-Ehrenberg 1984; Kharitonova 2004.

51. As is well observed by Dowden 1980:488–489.

52. For the problem of Iranian shamanism, see most recently Piras 2014.

53. For Mithras and Mithraism, see now the excellent new survey by Gordon 2012; Hensen 2013; Bremmer 2014.

54. Similarly, Dowden 1980:488–490.

55. For Abaris, see Dowden 2015a, note also Piras 2000.

56. Meuli 1975:2.859 ("Im Fall des andern skythischen Wundermannes").

57. See, most recently, Bremmer 2002b:691; Dana 2007.

58. Meuli 1975:2.879, cf. von Stuckrad 2003:108.

59. Meuli 1975:2.677–698 (*Kalevala*), 865 note 3 (interest), 1023–1033 (Orpheus) .

60. Mangani 1980; Russell 1981; Lloyd-Jones 1982; Cambiano 1991; a series of articles by Todd 1998, with the addenda in 2005; 1998; 2004; 2005; especially, Hankey 2007.

61. Dodds 1951.

62. See, most recently, Bremmer 2010b.

63. Burkert 1962, translated and revised in Burkert 1972; and 1962, reprinted in Burkert 2006. von Stuckrad 2003:112 n. 231 notes that I did not pay attention to this article in my previous studies of Greek shamanism. The present discussion is an attempt to remedy this neglect.

64. Burkert 2006:176 n. 17.

65. Herodotus 4.105, with Corcella *ad loc.*, cf. Buxton 2013:42.

66. Burkert 2006:179.

67. Burkert 2006:179–180.

68. Beekes 2010:1.280–281.

69. This is also insufficiently taken into account, in an attractive elaboration of Burkert's article, by Johnston 1999a, which is a "highly condensed and refocused version" (note 1) of Johnston 1999b.

70. Burkert 1985:180, 320, 446.

71. Burkert 1979:88–94; compare also Burkert 2002:6–7 on the Inanna/Ishtar myth, where he notes "allerdings hat es in den sumerischen Stadtstaaten und erst recht in der assyrischen Epoche gewiss keinen ausgebildeten Schamanismus mehr gegeben" (1982).

72. Burkert 2006:189–190.

73. For a full study of Aristeas' testimonia and texts, see Dowden 2015b; Tortorelli Ghidini 2015.

74. Robert 1990:213; Curbera 1997:92; Fraser and Matthews 2010:243. For the second part of the name, Norbert Oettinger (email

13-11-2014) writes to me: "... Jetzt aber halte ich die Verbindung von -bios mit normalem -pios, luwisch -piya- doch für richtig, denn ich habe bei Ph. Houwink ten Cate, *The Luwian Population Groups* (Leiden, 1965) 177 einen Arzybios (Kilikien) gefunden, wo dem b kein Nasal vorausgeht. Auch nennt I.J. Adiego, *The Carian Language* (Leiden, 2007) 332 neben Masaris, karischer Name des Dionysos, einen PN Masarabis. Und S. 339 aus Karien einen Neterbimos, der in der lykischen Triligue vom Letoon von Xantos als Natrbbijemis (mit Zirkumflex = Nasalierung über dem e) = Apollódotos erscheint. Im Lykischen gibt es kein Lautgesetz rp > rb, wie z.B. lyk. hrppi "für" (mit p) zeigt. Sonst gibt es in den epichorischen Inschriften der anatolischen Sprachen hier nirgends b, vielleicht weil p überall analogisch restituiert wurde. Melchert 2013:47 erwähnt kein b.

I guess now that -bi- instead of -pi- stems from examples like Tarkumbios, Ro:ndbie:s and Iambias where the development from p to b was regular. It spread then to other names like Kaystrobios by analogy. The analogy may have started within Anatolian languages itself as Lycian Natr-bbijemi (with *b) = Apollodotos shows".

75. Jacoby *ad FGrH* (34-)35, Addenda, overlooked by Bolton 1962:8–19; Ivantchik 1993 (around 500 BC); see also Burkert 1963:235 (first half of sixth century); Dan 2012:68–90 (second half of sixth century).

76. Garbounova 1997; d'Ercole 2009.

77. But note that West 2013:26 still dates Aristeas to the seventh century.

78. This is well stressed by West 2004:54–55, but not taken into account by Federico 2012.

79. Bolton 1962:174–175.

80. Iamblichus, *VP* 267.

81. One cannot escape the impression that Aristeas' spirit journey belongs more to the early Roman Empire than to Archaic Greece, cf. Lightfoot 2014:108 for parallels between Aristeas and Dionysius as described by Maximus of Tyre (X.2f-3c, XXXVIII.3c-g).

82. Bremmer 1983:24–48; Graf 1987:80–106, who has been overlooked by Afonasina 2007; Hadot 2001; Bremmer 2002:27–40, 145–51; Zhmud 2012.

83. To a certain extent, this is perhaps true, too, for the work of Carlo Ginzburg in relation to shamanism, on which see Kuiper 2004.

84. von Stuckrad 2003:106–116.

85. von Stuckrad 2003:114.

86. For a much more helpful approach, see Hutton 2006.

87. See the still valuable considerations of Geertz 1983:55–70; Ginzburg 2012b, reprinted in Ginzburg 2013g.

88. Gernet 1968:415–30 (1945) at 425, 429 (quotes).

89. Vernant 1971:110–111 ("shamane", "shamanisme").

90. Bremmer 2010b:18–22.

91. Mulsow 2012:317.

92. Bob Fowler (email 28-12-2014) comments: "I think what you say at the end about what brings all these shamanists together is right, and needed to be said; they are all revolutionaries who, though possessing profound classical learning, realised its isolationism and sought to open new avenues of research and establish new interpretative frameworks. Rohde too. But it can be added that both Wilamowitz, standing by to repel all foreign boarders, and the shamanists, eager to show that the boarders actually built the Greek ship in the first place, are fine examples of Orientalism: the exotic other is undifferentiated and reified".

93. Herodotus 3.116, with Asheri *ad loc.*; Ctesias *FGrH* 688 F 45, 45h; Pliny, *NH* 7.10, cf. Peissel 1984:144–149; Cardell, *Herodotus and the Gold Digging Ants* = https://www.academia.edu/12455298/Herodotus_and_the_gold_digging_ants_he_was_not_lying.

94. West 2007:22; Bremmer 2010b:19–20.

95. Cf. Oettinger 2015; see also, recently Egetmeyer 2007; Graf 2009.

96. West 2007:148–149 (Apollo), 345–347 (pillar).

97. Gernet 1968:425.

98. This is the somewhat revised and annotated version of my lecture at the Stockholm Colloquium "Horizons of Shamanism: A Triangular Approach" at the Stockholm History of Religions 100th anniversary

(1913–2013) on 8 November 2013. I am most grateful to Marjorie Mandelstam Balzer, Carlo Ginzburg and the Stockholm audience as well as to Bob Fowler, Yme Kuiper and Leonid Zhmud for enlightening discussions and comments. Richard Buxton insightfully corrected my English.

Afterword

Ulf Drobin
Stockholm University, Sweden

If we look back to the classical evolutionism of Spencer, Tylor, Frazer etc., and compare it with today's anthropology, the difference in time-depth is striking. To the early evolutionists, human culture was much younger than we know it to be today. Even still extant non-literate societies could be looked upon as reflecting preliminary stages in the history of mankind. This was a judgement made not just from the point of view of culture, but also from the point of view of cerebral development.

Proponents of the diffusionist trend in anthropology, folklore studies and historical philology believed that, when it came to chronology and geography, it was possible to reconstruct relatively correct maps of the historico-geographical distribution of different cultural phenomena. The exaggerated example of the Swedish folklorist Waldemar Liungman's *Traditionswanderungen Euphrat-Rhein* I and II and *Traditionswanderungen Rhein-Jennisei* I and II[1] comes to mind. After having read this extensive work, my conclusion is that it hardly concerns the migrations of general folk customs, but simply the migration of the art of writing and in particular the spread of printing. Even this is of course also an overstatement, because we have reasons to expect that the earliest testimonies have been lost. Still, the books have a tangible value in that they contain exhaustive descriptions of the presented folklore phenomena. What I consider "exaggerated" rather concerns the "Traditionswanderungen", i.e. the exact geographical mapping of the spread of the phenomena, in other words, the 'diffusionism'.

I should add that I do not believe that the spread of traditions in olden days can be reconstructed in "permanent migratory routes",

How to cite this book chapter:
Drobin, U. 2016. Afterword. In: Jackson, P. (ed.) *Horizons of Shamanism: A Triangular Approach to the History and Anthropology of Ecstatic Techniques.* Pp. 79–88. Stockholm: Stockholm University Press. DOI: http://dx.doi.org/10.16993/bag.f. License: CC-BY 4.0

i.e. as unilinear diffusion. Instead I propose that similar phenomena, for more or less similar reasons, have appeared over vast geographical areas and that every such place can be equated with a point of impact on water, with lots of rings created on the surface, and the observed running together in complicated and indescribable patterns within an even more extensive area.

If everything or at least most things have existed much earlier than was previously thought, it follows that phenomena in general are older than their earliest testimonies, but also that they were linked through much more complicated geographical relationships than can be proven today. To this can be added that conceptions considered to represent different periods in evolutionary terms are often seen to co-exist in the same societies, even to such an extent that it would have surprised a classical evolutionist. From the point of view of the history of ideas there is probably a certain reciprocity between evolutionism and diffusionism. Due to the accumulated knowledge of the difficulties surrounding 'historico-geographical' investigations – or what could almost be considered a synonym, 'historico-philological' investigations, since the sources are mostly written – interest for that kind of research has noticeably diminished. I am not proposing that historico-philological research should cease, but that one has to be aware of the whole world lying *beneath* the earliest testimonies. Absent proof of a phenomenon's preexistence is not a proof of its earlier inexistence. This means that when the historico-philological method has brought us to the end of documentation, it should be combined with an anthropological approach, i.e. one that in its general phenomenological view also takes the non-literate cultures into account and consideration. One should not make oneself comfortable with merely describing what one scientifically knows, for in practice this easily leads to treating phenomena whose existence cannot be proven as if they *de facto* never existed. Negative knowledge – not to know – changes into illusory positive knowledge – to know on false premises. Here my reservations concern the detailed accounts of the paths of geographical *diffusion*, and not so much the general phenomenological surveys describing the geographical distribution of different phenomena.

That said, I have somewhat truistically declared a sceptic attitude to diffusionistic investigations. The scepticism is directed, partly on different grounds, to both Bremmer, who in the question of shamanism attempts to deny a connection between Europe (predominantly Greece) and shamanism's so-called core area, and Ginzburg, who on the contrary seeks to confirm such a connection. The difference can be said to imply that Bremmer[2] is more excluding in his means to determine what really could be called shamanism than Ginzburg[3] is. Both emphasize the word 'shaman', in Bremmer's case to such an extent that his investigation tends to be a question of word history.

Ginzburg is very aware of the need to combine a historical research attitude with a structural one, equal to a morphological, i.e. a phenomenological, attitude.[4] However, an independent phenomenological research attitude can easily be reduced by the diffusionist outlook. I shall demonstrate this with Eliade's way of judging Old Norse *seiðr* (the Old Norse form of shamanism, in Swedish '*sejd*') in his "Shamanism, Archaic Techniques of Ecstasy",[5] a book which in many ways has received an almost normative function. Another book that, in my own and in many others' opinion, is very important was written in 1935 and in the same year was presented as a doctoral thesis: Dag Strömbäck's "Sejd. Textstudier i nordisk religionshistoria" [*Seiðr*. Text studies in Nordic History of Religion].[6] Strömbäck identifies *seiðr* with shamanism. The foremost practitioner of *seiðr* in Old Norse times was the god Óthin. Thus writes the Icelander Snorri Sturluson (1179–1241) in chapter 7 of the Ynglinga saga:

> "Óthin could shift his appearance. When he did so his body would lie there as if he were asleep or dead; but he himself, in an instant, in the shape of a bird or animal, a fish or a serpent, went to distant countries on his or other men's errands."[7]

Observe that Snorri's epic description of Óthin's skills is formulated nearly as if it were the modern and generally accepted definition of shamanism within the History of Religions.

The extensive work *Heimskringla; History of the Kings of Norway* consists of many parts, altogether making up 854 pages, beginning with the *Ynglinga saga* (the story of the royal lineage of the Ynglings). The entire work is considered to have been written sometimes between 1230 and 1240. This testimony of knowledge of shamanism might supply one of the oldest evidences of shamanism, after Herodotos' description of Scythian shamanism (regardless of one's evaluation of Herodotos' accuracy as a witness): should the direction of diffusion from Asia to Europe be reversed? Or is it simply impossible to imagine that the Old Norse case could concern real shamanism, especially when taking into account the distance between Northern Europe and the so-called core areas of shamanism in central Asia? It is here that Eliade comes into the picture. As a Scandinavian philologist myself I can affirm that Eliade was well acquainted with Old Norse material, and also with Dag Strömbäck's "Sejd".[8] In their basic outlook on the origin and diffusion of shamanism Ginzburg and Eliade stand rather close to each other. In his conclusion concerning the nature of Old Norse *seiðr*, Eliade maintains: "it is not shamanism in the strict sense but belongs to a horizon that is extremely close to it".[9] In my opinion his dictum depends less on the detailed, nearly "scholastically" elaborated definition of shamanism which he uses here than on the Nordic countries' location at the very geographical end of the imagined long diffusional chain. It seems natural to think that the intensity of the original features of a phenomenon would abate during a long geographical wandering. Eliade's conclusion has probably contributed to the striking dissension between Nordic scholars concerning the question as to what extent *seiðr* should be viewed as a form of shamanism or not. Diffusionism influences the phenomenological judgement.

But here I will go one step further regarding Eliade. My apprehension is that Eliade, with his stylistic brilliance and exceptional learning, led the research on shamanism astray by taking the very word 'shaman' as point of departure and hence getting stuck in the opinion that the *phenomenon* shamanism should have had its beginning where the *word* 'shaman' was first to be found. According to the same logic, shamanism should then have wandered widely over the world in many directions, and this principally in a scale of falling intensity of its characteristics according to the distance to the starting point. Why assume such a stable connection between word and phenomenon? And why should the beginning from the point of view of development be a culmination without prehistory?[10]

The discussion between Ginzburg and Bremmer concerns the now so well known benandanti, 'the good witches',[11] who during nightly dreams (*in spirito*), but nevertheless in a real world (!), i.e. in a spatial sense,[12] gather together to fight against 'the evil witches' in order to ensure fertility of the fields. The circumstances that the benandanti claim to travel in in their dreams, on hares, cats or other animals but nevertheless in some way within the sphere of reality, induces Ginzburg to associate them, in my eyes convincingly, with shamanism and shamanistic trance. The shaman can, as is well known, travel in the form of his free-soul to the realm of death, during which travel his body lies "as dead" on the place of the séance. But Ginzburg, as far as I know, does not discuss the phenomenological difference between benandanti and the shamanism as we know it from the so-called Asian core areas. However, he tries to strengthen his claim that real shamanism is at stake by providing a comprehensive account of the diffusion between what is believed to be the Asiatic area of origin and Italy, using evidence that has since long been considered secured by facts.

The events occurred, according to the records of the Inquisition, around the area of Friuli in Italy from 1570 to around the middle of the 17th century. According to Ginzburg, it was through the Inquisition's violent persecutions, whereby torture and bestial methods of killing were used, that confessions of putatively frightful satanic crimes were extorted. This was done in accordance with a then prevailing theological conceptual complex, which ultimately gave rise to the conception of the witches' Sabbath. These records from the Inquisition, in so far as we pay heed to the aims and worldview of the Inquisitors, can thus be treated as anthropological documents of outstanding depth and richness of details.

The exciting discussion between Ginzburg and Bremmer opens up trains of thought that, as far as I know, have not been expressed earlier. The notion that the conceptions of the soul should have evolved through influence from shamanism (or in this case that such conceptions among the ancient Greeks should have emerged through influence from Scythian shamanism) is rightly rejected by Bremmer as unthinkable.[13] The inverse course of events is generally seen as the more likely. Shamanism presupposes the conception of the free-soul. Dualistic pluralism seems in principle to exist/have existed among all peoples who remained outside the influence of the so-called high religions and seems in that respect to be more or less universal. Of course, all peoples have not been investigated, but I do not know of any investigated people that would confute this. These conceptions of the soul seem, possibly from very early periods onwards, to have represented religious phenomenological *elementa* in the same way as conceptions of gods, spirits, magic etc. can be said to have done. As a matter of fact, conceptions of the soul express elementary reflections on the conditions of life: the difference between dreaming and being awake, and between life and death as well as the psychological apprehension that within one there is something (life souls) which with a certain automatism steers one. This means that within the great diffusional area which both Ginzburg and Bremmer intersect there should once upon a time have been peoples with such conceptions of the soul more or less everywhere – and not only within the great diffusional area.

If one perceives the dream as an expression of the free-soul travelling beyond the body to remote geographical places and to other worlds (which is very well documented), then the step to shamanism is not far. Compare with shamanism the following quotation from "The Night Battles":

> "These benandanti say that when their spirit leaves the body it has the appearance of a mouse, and also when it returns, and that if the body should be rolled over while it is without its spirit, it would remain dead, and the spirit could never return to it." [14]

Shamanism means that by his own will the shaman, through a technique of ecstasy, tries to accomplish what is believed to take place in the dream, which means that shamanism could have developed everywhere where the conception of the free-soul has existed. Consequently, it is probable that in the era beyond documentation shamanism has flourished to a much larger extent than can be evidenced through historical or ethnographical modes of access. From this follows that what is now considered to be shamanism's core area can scarcely be regarded as the source of shamanism, but rather as the space that has retained it through historical coincidences.

One further remark: the many interesting archaic "mythologems" and "motifs", as one might metaphorically label this variety of narrative elements, which surface in Ginzburg's benandanti records and get connected with the shamanoid features need not to be considered to form an original organic entity. If it was, this outlook would be equal to a student fairy-tale research maintaining that a certain fairy tale, built up by a number of specific "motifs", constituted the original tale, an "Urmärchen" that always preserved the same components – a statement that would arouse surprise and sharp protests.[15] This should in principle also apply to different cultic elements' changing connections over the time axis. The shamanistic elements must, from the point of view of evolution, be considered independently of the other features, even if those features would seem to indicate the high age of the tale. On the other hand, such records of course have a special capacity to reflect the time and circumstances in which they were first written down.

I find the proposition that the benandanti really represent a form of shamanism highly convincing. It may be added that Eliade was fully convinced by this as well.[16] Nevertheless, Ginzburg's and Bremmer's diffusionistic deductions seem to me in both cases unlikely, because they presuppose that the benandanti either should have had or verifiably should not have had their utmost origin in the Asiatic so-called core areas of shamanism, a connection that Ginzburg attempts to confirm by showing that it really is a matter of shamanism and that Bremmer opposes with the contrary assertion, i.e. that it does not concern shamanism, or at least that there is no evidence to prove that it would be shamanism. In my opinion, a more probable scenario would be to understand the benandanti as representatives of rudimentary shamanism, as inheritors of an archaic remnant of a type of conception, which once, as a cultural undercurrent, might have been spread over vast areas, and now rises to the surface again through the medium of Ginzburg's investigations.

We may consider it to constitute a kind of pre- or protoshamanism. Shamanism ought also to have a developmental history, and to derive the "rudimentary" from the so-called core areas, which apparently contain the most elaborate forms of shamanism in terms of culture and thought, would imply that the benandanti represent a degenerated form of shamanism. This seems to me much more far-fetched than the opposite point of view. Looked upon from the "Stockholm perspective", the discovery of the benandanti appears even more epoch-making.

Finally, I want to emphasize that Ginzburg's benandanti research, beyond the discussion of the origin of shamanism, contains very important material that will certainly keep scholars busy for a long time. For instance, it throws new light on the enigmatic cult societies that Lily Weiser-Aall[17] and Otto Höfler[18] have written about. This is a fascinating topic that the former Docent (associate professor) at our Department, Andrejs Johansons (1922–1983), also treated.[19]

There is a picture – let us hope that it mostly is a distorted one – of anthropological field-work portraying the field-worker as someone who, in an imperialistic and cynically exploitive manner, makes an academic career at the expense of the native persons who he or she has interviewed and with whom the field-worker then cuts all ties as soon as possible. Marjorie Mandelstam Balzer presents a remarkably contrasting picture to this stereotype. In her field research she really shows human understanding and social engagement in an exemplary way. If the negative attitude of the field-worker is described as taking without giving anything back, then our Department's first field-worker, Åke Hultkrantz, must also be seen as exemplary. During the latter part of the 1940s and into the 1950s Hultkrantz carried out extensive field research among the Shoshone Indians in Wyoming, USA, where he amassed a wealth of material on their religion and culture, which was much more intact in those days. Around twelve years ago a delegation from the Shoshone and a film team spent several days at his home in Lidingö, outside Stockholm, to express their appreciation of his lifelong research and to make a film. Hultkrantz handed over his entire photo collection from his years of research from 1948 on-wards and gave the delegation and team glimpses of his unpublished field-work, which they knew contained many traditional events and phenomena that have now disappeared and are mostly forgotten. Much of the material has been translated to English and edited and compiled by his wife Geraldine. It was published in Wyoming under the title "Stories of Eastern Shoshone".[20]

In conclusion I should like to restate what Carlo Ginzburg mentions at the very beginning of his chapter that he has never met a shaman. This probably also applies to Jan Bremmer, as it does to me. Consequently, it is all the more important that one of the participants in the discussion has the experience that the others lack. We at the Department of the History of Religions are therefore very grateful that Marjorie Mandelstam Balzer was able to take up our invitation.

Notes

1. Liungman 1937; 1938; 1941; 1945.

2. Bremmer maintains, for example, that Herodotos' description of the Scythians' burial practices should not, as has been thought earlier for many years, be taken to show any evidence of shamanism. Bremmer 1983:25 ff. Compare Ginzburg 2004:207–225.

3. Carlo Ginzburg 2004. See Part Three, chap. 1: Eurasian Conjectures, pages 207–225.

4. Ginzburg 1993.

5. Eliade 1964.

6. Strömbäck 2000.

7. Snorri Sturluson. *Heimskringla. History of the Kings of Norway.* Translated with Introduction and Notes by Lee M. Hollander. 1964:10. In original language: Snorri Sturluson, *Heimskringla* I. Íslenzk fornrit. XXVI. Bindi. Reykjavík. MCMLXXIX. Chapter 7, page 1.

8. Mircea Eliade (as above), chapter eleven: Shamanic Ideologies and Techniques among the Indo-Europeans. Preliminary Remarks, Pages 375–387.

9. Mircea Eliade (as above), pages 386 f.

10. For a concise summary of Eliade's concept of shamanism, see Eliade 1987.

11. See Foreword, note 16.

12. A psychologist by profession would perhaps today try to use terms such as 'hypnopompic' and 'hypnagogic hallucinations' as an explanation.

13. Bremmer's lecture, page 12.

14. Ginzburg 2013c:18.

15. Thompson 1961; 1987; 1955–1958: 6 Vol.

16. Eliade 1978:78 ff.

17. Weiser 1927.

18. Höfler 1934; 1973.

19. Johansons 1973–1974:149–157. Ginzburg has read this article.

20. Hultkrantz 2009.

Response by Carlo Ginzburg

Carlo Ginzburg

In his "Afterword" Ulf Drobin commented on some works of mine, raising important points, both factual and methodological. I will try to answer his criticism starting from Kenneth Pike's well known distinction between *emic* and *etic* levels – designating, respectively, actors's and observer's categories. In *Storia notturna* (translated into English as *Ecstasies*) I did not mention Pike's dichotomy, although I was already familiar with it.[1] I will do it now, relying upon the reworking of Pike's argument I advanced in an essay entitled "Our Words and Theirs".[2]

Shaman is an *emic* word, shaman*ism* an *etic* concept. Different notions of shaman*ism* have been put forward by historians of religions and anthropologists: all of them imply a more or less wide distance (in terms of time, space and content) from the actual, recorded use of the word *shaman*. In *Ecstasies* I repeatedly mentioned the adjective "shamanistic" (sciamanistico), although I deliberately refrained – except in passages commenting on somebody else's works (for instance, Eliade's) – from using the abstract noun "shamanism" (sciamanesimo).[3] "Shamanism" is a scholarly construction, not a fact; our word, not theirs (as I would say today).

These remarks may introduce my answers to Drobin's criticism. I did not, as Drobin noted, "discuss the phenonomenological difference between the benandanti and the shamanism as we know it from the so-called Asian core areas" since the notion of "shamanism" did not play any role in my argument. Therefore, my attempt to identify a series of family resemblances across a very wide geographic area did not involve, *pace* Drobin, either the "claim that real shamanism" was at stake, or the inference that "the benandanti represent a degenerated form of shamanism". The effort made by Friulian inquisitors to convince the benandanti that they were not counter-witches, as they claimed, but real witches, took place in the framework of a historical clash, not as a degeneration of an evolutionary process.[4]

"We may consider [the benandanti beliefs as] a kind of pre- or proto-shamanism" Drobin writes: an interesting, although highly speculative suggestion – possibly even more speculative than the "Eurasian conjectures" which I chose as a title for the third part of *Ecstasies*. Those conjectures were based on an attempt to use morphological analogies as a tool to explore possible historical connections. Drobin noted that I have been "very aware of the need to combine a historical research attitude with a structural one, equal to a morphological, i. e. a phenomenological attitude". The last equation seems to me problematic: morphology works with configurations, phenomenology with isolated units. Therefore, when Drobin writes that "in their basic outlook on the origin and diffusion of shamanism Ginzburg and Eliade stand rather close to each other", I am perplexed. The interaction between morphology and history which was at the center of my research seems to me as distant as possible from Eliade's work, which is based on a tacit identification between phenomenology and history. "An independent phenomenological research attitude can easily be reduced to a diffusionist outlook" Drobin writes: an appropriate description of Eliade's approach. "Independent" phenomenology unfolds outside the constraints of history. Morphology, as I conceived it, submits itself to the constraints of history. On the one hand, identity; on the other, compatibilities. Different assumptions, different research strategies; different conclusions.

Notes

1. Ginzburg 1987:615–636 (especially p. 636, note 64); 1991b.

2. Ginzburg 2012b.

3. See for instance Ginzburg 1989:183 note 65; 1990:203 note 66.

4. Ginzburg 1966; 1983; new edition with a new introduction, 2013c.

Response by Jan N. Bremmer

Jan N. Bremmer

In his Afterword, Ulf Drobin raises some interesting questions, but they are, I fear, also insoluble ones. He rightly observes that our oldest evidence about shamanism is textual and thus limited in time. Although he concentrates on Ginzburg's *benandanti*, his observations are similarly valid for the problem of a possible Scythian shamanism. Here, as we have no other early sources, we can only work with Herodotus. In addition, we should also take into account that we have no early sources on Siberian shamanism, and Dobrin well notes that even Siberian shamanism must have known a historical development. Consequently, from a strictly methodological point of view it will be nearly impossible to say anything sensible about Scythian shamanism, as its content has to be filled in with data of shamanism of more than two millennia later. Yet Drobin's suggestion of a pre- or proto-shamanism as an etic concept to work with is attractive in connection with the *benandanti*. Friuli looks very much like a *Rückzugsgebiet*, where older ideas and practices survived much longer than in other, more accessible areas. For the study of Greek shamanism, though, such an idea is of no further help. Given our lack of sources, it seems more persuasive to take a skeptical stand as I have done in my various contributions on Greek shamanism.

References

Adiego, Ignatio J. 2007. *The Carian Language*. Leiden: Brill.

Afanas'ev, Lazar A. (Téris). 1993. *Aiyy yoreghe [Teachings of the spirit]*. Yakutsk: Ministry of Culture. [In Sakha].

Afonasina, Anna. 2007. 'Shamanism and the Orphic Tradition'. In *Skepsis* 18:24–31.

Alekseev, Nikolai A. 1984. *Shamanizm tiurkoiazychnykh narodov Sibiri*. Novosibirsk: Nauka.

Ancker, Estrid. 1962. *Torgny Segerstedt 1876–1945*. Stockholm: Tidens förlag.

Angelini, Pietro. 2007. 'Introduction'. In P. Angelini (ed.). *Dal laboratorio del 'Mondo magico': Carteggi 1940–1943*. Lecce: Argo, 9.

——— 2008. *Ernesto de Martino*. Roma: Carocci Editore.

Arbman, Ernst. 1922. *Rudra. Untersuchungen zum altindischen Glauben und Kultus*. Inauguraldissertation. Uppsala.

——— 1926–1927. *Untersuchungen zur primitiven Seelenvorstellung mit besonderer Rücksicht auf Indien*. Le Monde Oriental I–II. Uppsala: Almqvist & Wiksell.

——— 1963. *Ecstasy or Religious Trance. In the Experience of the Ecstatics and from the Psychological Point of View*. Volume I: Vision and Ecstasy. Uppsala: Svenska bokförlaget.

——— 1968. *Ecstasy or Religious Trance. In the Experience of the Ecstatics and from the Psychological Point of View*. Volume II: Essence and Forms of Ecstasy. Uppsala: Svenska bokförlaget.

——— 1970. *Ecstasy or Religious Trance. In the Experience of the Ecstatics and from the Psychological Point of View*. Volume III: Ecstasy and Psychopathological States. Uppsala: Svenska bokförlaget.

Atkinson, Jane Monnig. 1992. 'Shamanisms Today'. In *Annual Review of Anthropology* 21:307–330.

Avvakum, Protopope Petrovich. 1861. *Zhitīe protopopa Avvakuma, im samim napisannoe.* Petersburg: D.E. Kozhanchikova.

Balzer, Marjorie Mandelstam. 1996. 'Sacred Genders in Siberia: Shamans, Bear Festivals and androgyny'. In S. P. Ramet (ed.). *Gender Reversals and Gender Cultures: Anthropological and Historical Perspectives.* London: Routledge, 164–182.

——— 1999. *The Tenacity of Ethnicity: A Siberian Saga in Global Perspective.* Princeton: Princeton University Press.

——— 2012. *Shamans, Spirituality and Cultural Revitalization: Explorations in Siberia and Beyond.* New York: Palgrave-Macmillan.

Baron, Samuel H. (ed.). 1967. *The Travels of* Olearius *in Seventeenth-Century Russia.* Stanford: Stanford University Press.

Basilov, Vladimir N. 1978. 'Vestiges of Transvestism in Central-Asian Shamanism'. In V. Diószegi & M. Hoppál (eds.). *Shamanism in Siberia.* Budapest: Akadémiai Kiadó, 281–289.

——— 1997. 'Chosen by the Spirits' In M. M. Balzer (ed.). *Shamanic Worlds: Rituals and Lore of Siberia and Central Asia.* Armonk, New York, London: M. E. Sharpe, 3–48.

Baumgarten, Roland. 2012. 'Meuli, Karl. Schweizer Klass. Philologe und Religionswissenschaftler'. In *Der Neue Pauly.* Supplement 6. Stuttgart: J. B. Meztler, 814–815.

Beekes, Robert. 2010. *Etymological Dictionary of Greek.* 2 vols. Leiden: Brill.

Berglie, Per-Arne. 1983. *Gudarna stiger ned. Rituell besatthet hos sherpas och tibetaner.* English Summary: The Gods Descend. Ritual possesion among Sherpas and Tibetans. Stockholm Dissertations in Comparative Religion 2. Stockholm: Stockholm University.

de Blécourt, Willem. 2007a. 'The Return of the Sabbat: Mental Archaeologies, Conjectural Histories or Political Mythologies?'. In J. B.-O. Davies (ed.). *Palgrave Advances in Witchcraft Historiography.* Basingstoke and New York: Palgrave Macmillan, 125–145.

——— 2007b. 'A Journey to Hell: Reconsidering the Livonian "Werewolf"'. In *Magic, Ritual, and Witchcraft* II:49–67.

——— 2007c. 'Spuren einer Volkskultur oder Dämonisierung? Bemerkungen über Ginzburgs *Die Benandanti*'. In *Kea. Zeitschrift für Kulturwissenschaften* II:17–29.

Bleibtreu-Ehrenberg, Gisela. 1984. *Der Weibmann. Kultischer Geschlechtswechsel im Schamanismus*. Frankfurt: Fischer Taschenbuch Verlag.

Boekhoven, Jeroen W. 2011. *Genealogies of Shamanism: Struggles for Power, Charisma and Authority*. Groningen: Groningen University.

Bolton, James David P. 1962. *Aristeas of Proconnesus*. Oxford: Clarendon Press.

Bonjour, Edgar. 1994. 'Karl Meuli (16.9.1891–1.5.1968)'. In *Neue Deutsche Biographie* 17. Berlin: Duncker & Humblot, 264–265.

Brand(t), Adam. 1698. *Beschreibung der Chinesischen Reise welche vermittelst einer Zaaris. Besandschaft durch dero Ambassadeur, Herrn Isbrand Ao. 1693, 94, und 95, von Moscau über Gross-Ustiga Sibirien, dauren und durch die Mongolische Tartarey verrichtet worden, und was sich dabey begeben, aus selbst erfahrner Nachricht metgetheilet*. Hamburg: Bey Benjamin Schillern.

Bravina, Rosa I. 2005. *Kontseptsiia zhizni i smerti v kul'ture Etnosa: Na Materiale Traditsii Sakha*. Yakutsk: YaGU.

Bremmer, Jan. 1983. *The Early Greek Concept of the Soul*. Princeton and London: Princeton University Press.

——— 2002a. *The Rise and Fall of the Afterlife*. London and New York: Routledge.

——— 2002b. 'Zalmoxis'. In *Der Neue Pauly* 12 (2). Stuttgart and Weimar: Metzler, 691.

——— 2010a. 'The Greek Gods in the Twentieth Century'. In J. Bremmer & A. Erskine (eds.). *The Gods of Ancient Greece*. Edinburgh: Edinburgh University Press, 1–18.

——— 2010b. 'The Rise of the Unitary Soul and its Opposition to the Body. From Homer to Socrates'. In L. Jansen & Ch. Jedan (eds.). *Philosophische Anthropologie in der Antike*. Frankfurt: Ontos, 11–29.

——— 2014. *Initiation into the Mysteries of the Ancient World*. Berlin and Boston: Walter de Gruyter.

Brown, Michael. 1988. 'Shamanism and its Discontents'. In *Medical Anthropology Quarterly* 2:102–120.

———— 1989. 'Dark Side of the Shaman'. In *Natural History* 11:8–10.

———— 2003. *Who Owns Native Culture?* Cambridge: Harvard University Press.

———— 2007. 'Sovereignty's Betrayals'. In M. de la Cadena *et al.* (eds.). *Indigenous Experience Today.* Durham: Duke University Press, 171–194.

Brown, Joseph Epes. 2007. *The Spiritual Legacy of the American Indian.* Bloomington: World Wisdom.

Brown, Joseph Epes & Emily Cousins. 2001. *Teaching Spirits: Understanding Native American Religious Tradition.* New York: Oxford University Press.

Burkert, Walter. 1962. *Weisheit und Wissenschaft: Studien zu Pythagoras, Philolaos und Platon.* Nuremberg: Hans Carl.

———— 1962. 'Γόης: Zum griechischen "Schamanismus"'. In *Rheinisches Museum* 105:36–55.

———— 1963. 'Review of Bolton, 1962'. In *Gnomon* 35:235–240.

———— 1972. *Lore and Science in Ancient Pythagoreanism.* Cambridge Massachusetts: Harvard University Press.

———— 1979. *Structure and History in Greek Mythology and Ritual.* Berkeley, Los Angeles, London: University of California Press.

———— 1985. *Greek Religion.* Oxford: Blackwell.

———— 2002. *Kleine Schriften II.* F. Graf (ed.). Göttingen: Vandenhoeck & Ruprecht.

———— 2006. *Kleine Schriften III.* F. Graf (ed.). Göttingen: Vandenhoeck & Ruprecht.

Buxton, Richard. 2013. *Myths and Tragedies in their Ancient Greek Contexts.* Oxford: Oxford University Press.

Buyandelger, Manduhai. 2013. *Tragic spirits: shamanism, memory, and gender in contemporary Mongolia.* Chicago and London: The University of Chicago Press.

Bäckman, Louise. 2013. *Samlade studier i samisk religion.* Stockholm history of religions centennial series 1. Stockholm: Stockholm University.

Bäckman, Louise & Hultkrantz, Åke. 1978. *Studies in Lapp Shamanism*. Acta Universitatis Stockholmiensis, Stockholm Studies in Comparative Religion 16. Stockholm: Stockholm University.

Bähr, Johan Christian Felix, *et al.* 1857. *Herodoti Musae*. Vol. 2. Leipzig: Hahn.

de la Cadena, Marisol, Orin Starn, (eds.). 2007. *Indigenous Experience Today*. Durham: Duke University Press.

Cambiano, Guiseppe. 1991. 'Eric Dodds: entre psychanalyse et parapsychologie'. In *Revue de l'histoire des religions* 208:3–26.

Cardell, Monique. 'Herodotus and the Gold Digging Ants' = https://www.academia.edu/12455298/Herodotus_and_the_gold_digging_ants_.he_was_not_lying.

Carpenter, Edmund S. 1961. 'Witch-Fear Among the Aivilik Eskimos'. In Yehudi A. Cohen (ed.). *Social Structure and Personality*. New York: Holt, Rhinehart and Winston, 508–515.

Casadio, Giovanni. 2014. *Lo sciamanesimo prima e dopo Eliade*. Rome: Il Calamo.

Charuty, Giodana. 2009. *Ernesto De Martino: Les vies antérieures d'un anthropologue*. Marseille: Parenthéses Parcours Méditerranéens.

Chirkova, Alexandra. 2002. *Shaman: Zhizn' i Bessmertie*. Yakutsk: Sakhapoligrafizdat.

Criukshank, Julie, Tatiana Argunova. 2000. 'Reinscribing Meaning: Memory and Indigenous Identity in Sakha Republic (Yakutia)'. In *Arctic Anthropology* 37 (1):96–119.

Csordas, Thomas. 2002. *Body/Meaning/Healing*. New York: Palgrave Macmillan.

Curbera, Jaime B. 1997. 'The Greek curse tablets of Emporion'. In *Zeitschrift für Papyrologie und Epigraphik* 117:92.

Dan, Anca. 2012. 'Quand Apollon portait en vol au-delà des Scythes'. In *Aristeas* (Moscow) 6:68–90.

Dana, Dan. 2007. 'Zalmoxis et la quête de l'immortalité: pour la révision de quelques théories récentes'. In *Les Études Classiques* 75:93–110.

Daschke, Dereck and Ashcraft, W. Michael (eds.). 2005. *New Religious Movements*. New York: New York University Press.

Delaby, Laurence. 1977. *Chamanes Toungouses*. Paris: Nanterre.

Diels, Hermann. 1897. *Parmenides*. Berlin: Reimer.

———— 1922. 'Himmels- und Höllenfahrten von Homer bis Dante'. In *Neue Jahrbücher für das klassische Altertum* 49:239–253.

———— 1969. *Kleine Schriften zur Geschichte der antiken Philosophie*. Hildesheim: Wissenschaftliche Buchgesellschaft.

Dodds, Eric R. 1951. *The Greeks and the Irrational*. Berkeley: University of California Press.

Dowden, Ken. 1980. 'Deux notes sur les Scythes et les Arimaspes'. In *REG* 93:486–492.

———— 2015a. 'Abaris (34)'. In *Brill's New Jacoby*. Brill Online.

———— 2015b. 'Aristeas (35)'. In *Brill's New Jacoby*. Brill Online.

van Eeghen, Isabella Henriette. 1978. *De Amsterdamse boekhandel 1680–1725*. Vol. 2. Amsterdam: Scheltema & Holkema.

Egetmeyer, Markus. 2007. 'Lumière sur les loups d'Apollon'. In *Res Antiquae* 4:205–220.

Eliade, Mircea. 1946. 'Le problème du chamanisme'. In *Revue de l'histoire des religions* 131:5–52.

———— 1951. *Le chamanisme et les techniques archaïques de l'extase*. Paris: Payot.

———— 1964, 1974, 2004. *Shamanism: Archaic Techniques of Ecstasy*. Princeton: Princeton University Press.

———— 1975. 'Some Observations on European Witchcraft'. In *History of Religions* 14:149–172.

———— 1978. *Das Okkulte und die moderne Welt. Zeitströmungen in der Sicht der Religionsgeschichte*. Salzburg: Müller.

———— 1987. Shamanism: an Overview. In *Encyclopaedia of Religion. Second Edition*. London, New York: Macmillan, 8269–8274.

d'Ercole, Maria Cecilia. 2009. 'Arimaspes et griffons, de la Mer Noire à l'Adriatique *via* Athènes'. In *Mètis* NS 7:203–225.

Federico, Eduardo. 2012. 'Erodoto, Aristea e la terra oltre gli Issedoni. Un'etnografia "estatica" al vaglio dell'historie'. In *Mythos* N.S. 6:9–21.

Ferrari, Fabrizio M. 2012. *De Martino on Religion: The Crisis and the Presence*. Sheffield: Equinox Publishing.

Flaherty, Gloria. 1992. *Shamanism and the Eighteenth Century*. Princeton: Princeton University Press.

Fortun, Kim; Fortun, Mike; Rubenstein, Steven (eds.). 2010. 'Emerging Indigeneities'. In *Cultural Anthropology* 25 (2):222–370.

Fowler, Robert L. 2009. 'Blood for the Ghosts: Wilamowitz in Oxford'. In *Syllecta Classica* 20:171–213.

Fraser, Peter & Matthews, Elaine. 2010. *A Lexicon of Greek Personal Names*. Vol. V. T. Corsten (ed.). Oxford: Clarendon Press.

Garbounova, X. 1997. 's.v. Arimaspoi'. In *Lexicon Iconographicum Mythologiae Classsicae* VIII, 1:529–534.

Geertz, Clifford. 1983. *Local Knowledge*. New York: Fontana.

Gellner, David N. 1994. 'Priests, Healers, Mediums and Witches: The Context of Possession in the Katmandu Valley, Nepal'. In *Man* 29:27–48.

Gernet, Louis. 1968. *Anthropologie de la Grèce antique*. Paris: Maspéro.

Ginzburg, Carlo. [1961] 2013a. 'Witchcraft and Popular Piety: Notes on a Modenese Trial of 1519'. In C. Ginzburg (ed.). *Clues, Myths, and the Historical Method*. Baltimore: John Hopkins University Press, 1–14.

––––––– 1972. *I benandanti. Stregoneria e culti agrari tra Cinquecento e Seicento*. Torino: Einaudi.

––––––– [1979a] 2013b. "Clues: Roots of an Evidential Paradigm". In C. Ginzburg (ed.). *Clues, Myths, and the Historical Method*. Baltimore: John Hopkins University Press, 87–113.

––––––– 1979b. '"La fine del mondo" di Ernesto de Martino'. In *Quaderni storici* 40:238–242.

––––––– 1981. *Indagini su Piero: Il Battesimo, il ciclo di Arezzo, la Flagellazione di Urbino*. Torino: Einaudi.

———— 1983, 2013c. *The Night Battles. Witchcraft and Agrarian Cults in the Sixteenth and Seventeenth Centuries*. Baltimore: John Hopkins University Press.

———— [1985a] 2013d. 'Freud, the Wolf-Man, and the Werewolves'. In C. Ginzburg (ed.). *Clues, Myths, and the Historical Method*. Baltimore: John Hopkins University Press, 132–140.

———— 1985b. *The Enigma of Piero. Piero della Francesca: The Baptism, The Arezzo Cycle, The Flagellation*. London: Verso.

———— 1987. Saccheggi rituali. Premesse a una ricerca in corso. Seminario bolognese coordinato da C.G. In «Quaderni storici» (65), 615–636.

———— 1988a. 'Momigliano e de Martino'. In *Rivista storica italiana* 100:400–413.

———— [1988b] 2013e. 'The Inquisitor as Anthropologist'. In C. Ginzburg (ed.). *Clues, Myths, and the Historical Method*. Baltimore: John Hopkins University Press, 141–148.

———— 1989. *Storia Notturna. Una decifrazione del sabba*. Turin: Einaudi.

———— 1991a. *Ecstasies: Deciphering the Witches' Sabbath*. New York: University of Chicago Press.

———— 1991b. *Benandanti. De goda häxmakarna*. Stockholm: Symposion.

———— 1991c. Ritual Pillages: A Preface to Research in Progress. A seminar coordinated by C. G. In E. Muir and G. Ruggiero (eds.). *Microhistory and the Lost People of Europe*. Baltimore: John Hopkins University, 20–41.

———— 1992. 'Gli Europei scoprono (o riscoprono) gli sciamani'. In F. Graf (ed.). *Klassische Antike und neue Wege der Kulturwissenschaften. Symposium Karl Meuli*. Basel: Verlag der Schweizerischen Gesellschaft für Volkskunde, 111–128.

———— 1993. 'Witches and Shamans'. In *New Left Review* 200 (July-August):75–85.

———— 2004. *Ecstasies: Deciphering the Witches' Sabbath*. Translated by Raymond Rosenthal. The University of Chicago Press edition.

————2010.'MirceaEliade'sAmbivalentLegacy'.InC.K.Wedemeyer&
W. Doniger (eds.). *Hermeneutics, Politics, and the History of
Religions: The Contested Legacies of Joachim Wach & Mircea
Eliade*. Oxford and New York: Oxford University Press, 307–323.

———— 2012a. *Threads and Traces: True False Fiction*. Berkeley, Los
Angeles, London: University of California Press.

———— 2012b. 'Our Words, and Theirs: A Reflection on the
Historian's Craft, Today'. In S. Fellman and M. Rahikainen (eds.).
Historical Knowledge: In Quest of Theory, Method and Evidence.
Cambridge: Cambridge Scholars Publishing, 97–119.

———— 2013f. 'German Mythology and Nazism: on an Old Book
by Georges Dumézil'. In C. Ginzburg (ed.). *Clues, Myths, and the
Historical Method*. Baltimore: John Hopkins University Press, 114.

———— 2013g. 'Our Words, and Theirs: A Reflection on the
Historian's Craft, Today'. In *Cromohs* (*Cyber Review of Modern
Historiography*) 18:97–114.

Ginzburg, Eugenia Semyonovna. 1981. *Within the Whirlwind*. 2nd
vol. Trans. H. Boll, L. Vennevitz. New York: Harcourt, Brace
Jovanovich.

Gogolev, Anatoly. 1993. *Yakuty: Problemy etnogenez i formirovaniia
kul'tury*. Yakutsk: Ministry of Culture.

———— 2002. *Istoki mifologii i traditsionnyi kalendar' Yakutov*.
Yakutsk: Ministry of Culture, Obrazovanie.

Gordon, Richard. 2012. 'Mithras'. In *Reallexikon der Antike
Christentum* 24:964–1009.

Graf, Fritz. 1987. 'Orpheus: A Poet among Men'. In J. Bremmer (ed.).
Interpretations of Greek Mythology. London: Routledge, 80–106.

———— 2009. *Apollo*. London and New York: Routledge.

Grant, Bruce. 2009. *The Captive and the Gift: Cultural Histories of
Sovereignty in Russia and the Caucasus*. Cornell University Press.

Grigoryants, Sergei. 1989. 'Camps with white Gowns'. In *Glasnost*
16–18 (January):34–47.

Hadot, Pierre. 2001. 'Shamanism and Greek Philosophy'. In H.-P.
Francfort and R.N. Hamayon (eds.). *The Concept of Shamanism:
Uses and Abuses*. Budapest: Akadémiai Kiadó, 389–401.

Handler, Richard. 2004. 'Afterword: Mysteries of Culture'. In *American Anthropologist* 106 (3):488–494.

Hankey, Wayne J. 2007. 'Re-evaluating E.R. Dodds' Platonism'. In *Harvard Studies in Classical Philology* 103:499–541.

Harner, Michael J. 2013. *Cave and cosmos: shamanic encounters with another reality*. Berkeley and California: North Atlantic Books.

Harvilahti, Lauri. 2000. 'Altai Oral Epic'. In *Oral Tradition* 15:215–229.

Hedin, Christer. 2013. *Ingenting är anstötligare än sanningen. Religion och politik hos Segerstedt*. Stockholm: Molin & Sorgenfrei.

Henrichs, Albert. 1985 '"Der Glaube der Hellenen": Religionsgeschichte als Glaubensbekenntnis und Kulturkritik', in W. M. Calder III *et al.* (eds.). *Wilamowitz nach 50 Jahren*. Darmstadt: Wissenschaftliche Buchgesellschaft, 262–305.

——— 1992. 'Gott, Mensch, Tier: Antike Daseinsstruktur und religiöses Verhalten im Denken Karl Meulis'. In F. Graf (ed.). *Klassische Antike und neue Wege der Kulturwissenschaften. Symposium Karl Meuli*. Basel: Verlag der Schweizerischen Gesellschaft für Volkskunde, 129–67.

Hensen, Andreas. 2013. *Mithras. Der Mysterienkult am Limes, Rhein und Donau*. Darmstadt: Theiss.

Herder, Johan Gottfried. 1807. *Sämmtliche Werke zur schönen Literatur und Kunst*. Vol. 8. Tübingen: Müller.

Hicks, David. 2010. *Ritual and Belief: Readings in the Anthropology of Religion*. Lanham and Maryland: Rowman and Littlefield, Alta-Mira Press.

Hoppál, Mihály. 1992. 'Urban Shamans, A Cultural Revival in a Postmodern World'. In *Studies on Shamanism*. Etnologica Uralica 2. Helsinki: Finnish Anthropological Society; Budapest: Akademiai Kiado, 197–209.

Houwink ten Cate, Philo. 1965. *The Luwian Population Groups of Lycia and Cicilia Aspera during the Hellenistic Period*. Leiden: Brill.

Hultkranz, Åke. 1953. *Conceptions of the Soul among North American Indians*. Statens Etnografiska Museum, Monograph Series. Publication No. 1. Stockholm: Ethnological Museum of Sweden.

———— 1983. *The Study of American Indian Religions*. New York: Crossroad.

———— 1991 'The Drum in Shamanism. Some reflections'. In T. Ahlbäck and J. Bergman (eds.). *The Saami Shaman Drum*. Scripta Instituti Donneriani Aboensis. Vol. XIV. Åbo and Stockholm, 9–27.

———— 1992. *Shamanic Healing and Ritual Drama*. New York: Crossroad.

———— 1997. *The Attraction of Peyote*. Stockholm: Almquist and Wiksell.

———— 2009. *Stories of the Eastern Shoshone. Told by John Trehero to Åke Hultkrantz. Transcribed, translated and edited by Geraldine Hultkrantz*. Lander, Wyoming: Mortimer publishing.

Humphrey, Caroline. 1999. 'Shamans in the City'. In *Anthropology Today* 15 (3):3–10.

Hundt, Michael. 1999. *Beschreibung der dreijährigen Chinesischen Reise: die Russische Gesandtschaft von Moskau nach Peking 1692 bis 1695 in den Darstellungen von Eberhard Isbrand Ides und Adam Brand*. Stuttgart: Steiner.

Hutton, Ronald. 2001. *Shamanism: Siberian Spirituality and the Western Imagination*. London and New York: Hambledon & London.

———— 2006. 'Shamanism: Mapping the Boundaries'. In *Magic, Ritual and Witchcraft* 1:209–213.

Hyde, Lewis. 1998. *Trickster Makes this World: Mischief, Myth, and Art*. New York: Farrar, Straus, and Giroux.

Höfler, Otto. 1934. *Kultische Geheimbünde der Germanen*. Frankfurt am Main: Diesterweg.

———— 1973. *Verwandlungskulte, Volkssagen und Mythen*. Wien: Verlag der Österreichischen Akademie der Wissenschaft.

Ivantchik, Askold. 1993. 'La datation du poème l'*Arimaspée* d'Aristéas de Proconnèse'. In *L'Antiquité Classique* 62:35–67.

Johansons, Andrejs. 1973–74. Kultverbände und Verwandlungskulte. In Arv. Tidskrift för nordisk Folkminnesforskning (Journal of Scandinavian folklore). 29–30:149–157.

Johnston, Sarah Iles. 1999a. 'Songs for the ghosts: Magical solutions to deadly problems'. In D. Jordan *et al.* (eds.). *The world of ancient magic*. Bergen: Norwegian Institute at Athens, 83–102.

———— 1999b. *Restless Dead*. Berkeley, Los Angeles, London: University of California Press.

Jung, Carl G. 1928. *Two Essays in Analytic Psychology*. New York: Dodd and Mead.

Kazanin, Mark Isaakovich (ed.). 1967. *Izbrant Ides i Adam Brant. Zapiski o russkom posol'stve v Kitaj (1692–1695)*. Moscow: Nauka.

Kendall, Laurel. 2009. *Shamans, Nostalgias, and the IMF: South Korean Popular Religion in Motion*. Honolulu: University of Hawaii Press.

Kharitonova, Valentina. 2004. 'Transvestism in Shamanism'. In M.N. Walter and E.J. Neumann Fridman (eds.). *Shamanism: An Encyclopedia of World Beliefs, Practices, and Culture*. 2 vols. Santa Barbara: ABC Clio, 1.259–263.

Klaniczay, Gábor. 2010. 'A Cultural History of Witchcraft'. In *Magic, Ritual and Witchcraft* 5:188–210.

Klingemann, Carsten. 2009. *Soziologie und Politik. Sozialwissenschaftliches Expertenwissen im Dritten Reich und in der frühen Westdeutschen Nachkriegszeit*. Wiesbaden: VS Verlag.

Knüppel, Michael. 2010. 'Nochmals zu alttürkisch šaman'. In *Zeitschrift für Religions- und Geistesgeschichte* 62:77–80.

Kolodesnikov, Sergei K. 2000. 'The person in the Traditional Yakut (Sakha) worldview.' In *Anthropology and Archeology of Eurasia* 39 (1):42–79.

Kondakov, Vladimir A. 1992. *Emteehin kistelengneritten [About a few secrets of folk curing]*. Yakutsk: Sakha Republic Association of Folk Medicine. [in Sakha].

———— 1993. *Dobyn khallaan byyhyn* [Sky's power brings health]. Yakutsk: Association of Folk Medicine. [in Sakha].

———— 1997. *Aiyy oiuuna* [White Shaman]. Yakutsk: Soruk Press. [in Sakha].

—— 1999. *Tainy sfery shamanizma*. Yakutsk: Aiyy Archyta.

—— 2005. *Algystar: Én Komuskélléring* [Prayer-Blessings: To Protect You]. Yakutsk: Scientific Center for Sakha Republic Association of Folk Medicine. [in Sakha].

Koss-Chioino, Joan D. 2006. 'Spiritual Transformation and Radical Empathy in Ritual Healing and Therapeutic Relationships'. In J. D. Koss-Chioino & Ph. Hefner (eds.). *Spiritual transformation and healing: anthropological, theological, neuroscientific, and clinical perspectives*. Lanham and Maryland: Alta Mira Press, 45–61.

Krippner, Stanley. 2000. 'The Epistemology and Technologies of Shamanic States of Consciousness'. In *Journal of Consciousness Studies* 7 (11/12):93–118.

Ksenofontov, Gavril V. [1928–9] 1992. *Shamanizm: Izbrannye trudy*. A.N. Diachkova (ed.). Yakutsk: Sever-Iug. for Museum of Music and Folklore.

Kuiper, Yme B. 2004. 'Witchcraft, Fertility Cults, and Shamanism: Carlo Ginzburg's *I benandanti* in Retrospect'. In B. Luchesi & K. von Stuckrad (eds.). *Religion in Cultural Discourse, Essays in Honor of Hans G. Kippenberg on the Occasion of His 65th Birthday*. New York and Berlin: de Gruyter, 34–59.

Kulakovsky, Alexei E. 1979. *Nauchnyie Trudy* [Scientific Studies]. Yakutsk: AN. Yakutskoe Knizhnoe Izdatel'stvo.

Kupferschmidt, Franz. 1935. *Karl Neumann: ein Beitrag zur Geschichte der wissenschaftlichen Geographie im 19. Jahrhundert*. Leipzig: Leipzig University.

Köhler, Marcus. 2012. *Russische Ethnographie und Imperiale Politik im 18. Jahrhundert*. Göttingen: V & R Unipress.

Latour, Bruno. 2002. *Iconoclash: Beyond the Image Wars in Science, Religion and Art*. Boston: MIT Press.

—— 2009. 'Perspectivism: Type or Bomb?' In *Anthropology Today* 25 (2):1–2.

Leibniz, Gottfried Wilhelm. 1979. *Novissima Sinica (1697): Das Neueste von China*. Translated by H.-G. Nesselrath & H. Reinbothe (eds.). Bonn-Oedekoven: Köllen Druck.

——— 1993. *Sämtliche Schriften und Briefe XIV*. Berlin: Akademie Verlag Berlin.

——— 2010. *Novissima Sinica (1697): Das Neueste von China*. Reprinted with bibliographical updates by G. Paul and A. Grünert. Munich: Nesselrath.

Lieber, Elinor. 1996. 'The Hippocratic "Airs, Waters, Places" on Cross-dressing Eunuchs: "Natural" yet also "Divine"'. In R. Wittern & P. Pellegrin (eds.). *Hippokratische Medizin und antike Philosophie*. Hildesheim: Olms, 451–476.

Lightfoot, Jane. 2014. *Dionysius Periegetes, Description of the Known World*. Oxford: Oxford University Press.

Lindquist, Galina & Coleman, Simon (eds.). 2008. 'Against Belief?'. In *Social Analysis* 52 (1):1–18.

Lloyd-Jones, Hugh. 1982. *Blood for the Ghosts*. London: Duckworth.

Lobeck, Christian August. 1829. *Aglaophamus*. Vol. 1. Königsberg: Borntraeger.

Liungman, Waldemar. 1937. *Traditionswanderungen Euphrat- Rhein. Studien zur Geschichte der Volksbräuche I*. FF Communications. No. 118. Helsinki.

——— 1938. *Traditionswanderungen Euphrat-Rhein. Studien zur Geschichte der Volksbräuche II*. FF Communications. No. 119. Helsinki 1938..

——— 1941. *Traditionswanderungen Rhein-Jenissei. Eine Untersuchung über das Winter- und Todaustragen und einige hierhergehörige Bräuche I*. FF Communications. No. 129. Helsinki.

——— 1945. *Traditionswanderungen Rhein-Jenissei. Eine Untersuchung über das Winter- und Todaustragen und einige hierhergehörige Bräuche II*. FF Communications. No. 131. Helsinki.

Lyon, William. 2012. *Spirit Talkers: North American Indian Medicine Powers*. Kansas City: Prayer Efficacy Publishing.

Mangani, Giorgio. 1980. 'Sul metodo di Eric Dodds e sulla nozione di "irrazionale"'. In *Quaderni di Storia* 11:173–205.

Marcus, George & Clifford, James (eds.). 1988. *New Directions in Anthropological Writing: History, Poetics, Cultural Criticism*. Madison: University of Wisconsin Press.

de Martino, Ernesto. 1941. *Naturalismo e storicismo nell'etnologia*. Bari: Latertza.

——— 1942a. 'Recensione'. In *Studi e materiali di storia delle religioni*, XVIII:108–111.

——— 1942b. 'Percezione extrasensoriale e magismo etnologico. In *Studi e materiali di storia delle religioni*, XVIII:1–19.

——— 1943–1946. 'Percezione extrasensoriale e magismo etnologico'. In *Studi e materiali di storia delle religioni*, XIX–XX:31–84.

———1948. *Il mondo magico: Prolegomeni a una storia del magismo*, Torino: Bollati Boringhieri.

——— 1953. 'Etnologia e cultura nazionale'. In *Società*, IX:314–315.

——— 1972. *Primitive Magic: the Psychic Powers of Shamans and Sorcerers*. Bay Books: Australia.

——— 1988, 1990, 1999. *Primitive Magic: The Psychic Powers of Shamans and Sorcerers*. Bridport and Dorset: Prism Press.

Mehl-Madrona, Lewis. 1997. *Coyote Medicine*. New York: Scribner.

Melchert, Craig. 2013. 'Naming Practices in 2nd and 1st Millenium Western Anatolia'. In R. Parker (ed.). *Personal Names of Ancient Anatolia*. Proceedings of the British Academy 191. Oxford: Oxford University Press, 31–50.

Merkur, Daniel. 1985. *Becoming Half Hidden: Shamanism and Initation Among the Inuit*. Acta Universitatis Stockholmiensis, Stockholm Studies in Comparative Religion 24. Stockholm: Stockholm University.

Meuli, Karl. 1935. 'Scythica'. In *Hermes* 70:121–176.

——— 1975. *Gesammelte Schriften*. 2 vols. Basel: Schwabe & Co., 2.1153–1209.

Michel, Ute. 1991. 'Wilhelm Emil Mühlmann (1904–1988) – ein deutscher Professor. Amnesie und Amnestie: Zum Verhältnis von Ethnologie und Politik im Nationalsozialismus'. In *Jahrbuch für Soziologie-Geschichte* 1991:69–117.

Mills, Antonia & Slobodin, Richard (eds.). 1994. *Amerindian Rebirth: Reincarnation Belief among North American Indians and Inuit*. Toronto: University of Toronto Press.

Mooney, James. 1991. *The Ghost-dance Religion and the Sioux outbreak of 1891*. Lincoln: University of Nebraska Press.

Mühlmann, Wilhelm Emil. 1936. *Rassen- und Völkerkunde. Lebensprobleme der Rassen, Gesellschaften und Völker*. Brauschweig: Vieweg.

———— 1937. 'Geschichtliche Bedingungen, Metoden und Aufgaben der Völkerkunde'. In Th. Preuss (ed.). *Lehrbuch der Völkerkunde*. Stuttgart: Ferdinand Enke, 1–43.

———— 1938. *Methodik der Völkerkunde*. Stutttgart: Ferdinand Enke.

———— 1940. 'Nachruf auf S. M. Sirokogorov (nebst brieflichen Erinnerungen)'. In *Archiv für Anthropologie, Völkerforschung und kolonialen Kulturwandel*. N. F. B. XXVI:55–64.

———— 1964. *Chiliasmus und Nativismus. Studien zur Psychologie, Soziologie und historischen Kasuistik der Umsturzbewegungen*. 2nd ed. Berlin: Dietrich Reimer.

———— 1968. *Geschichte der Anthropologie*. Zweite verbesserte und erweiterte Auflage. Frankfurt am Main-Bonn: Athenäum Verlag.

Müller, Kurt. 1955. 'Gottfried Wilhelm Leibniz und Nicolaas Witsen'. In *DSB Deutsche Akademie der Wissenschaft zu Berlin*, vol. 1. Berlin: Akademie Verlag Berlin.

Mulsow, Matrin. 2012. *Prekäres Wissen*. Berlin: Suhrkamp Verlag.

Nadasdy, Paul. 2007. 'The Gift in the Animal: The Ontology of Hunting and Human-Animal Sociality'. In *American Ethnologist* 34 (1):25–43.

Nagel, Joane. 1996. *American Indian Ethnic Renewal: Red Power and the Resurgence of Identity and Culture*. Oxford: Oxford University Press.

Nanninga, Rob. 2002. *Cults and New Religious Movements: A Bibliography*. University of Florida.

Narby, Jonathan, Huxley, Francis (eds.). 2001. *Shamans Through Time: 500 Years on the Path to Knowledge*. New York: Putnam.

Neumann, Karl. 1852. *De rebus Olbiopolitanorum*. Königsberg: Königsberg University.

———— 1855. *Die Hellenen im Skythenlande*. Vol. 1. Berlin: Georg Reimer.

Nilsson, Martin P. [1937] 1963. *Helvetets förhistoria. Straff och sällhet i den andra världen i förkristen religion*. Lund: Aldus.

Oettinger, Norbert. 2015. Apollo: indogermanisch oder nicht-indogermanisch? In *Münchener Studien zur Sprachwissenschaft* 69, 123–143.

Paulson, Ivar. 1958. *Die primitiven Seelenvorstellungen der nordeurasischen Völker. Eine religionsethnographische und religionsphänomenologische Untersuchung*. The Etnographical Museum of Sweden (Statens Etnografiska Museum). Monograph Series. Publication No 5. Stockholm: Etnographical Museum of Sweden.

———— 1961. *Schutzgeister und Gottheiten des Wildes (der Jagdtiere und Fische) in Nordeurasien. Eine religionsethnographische Untersuchung jägerischer Glaubens- vorstellungen*. Acta Universitatis Stockholmiensis, Stockholm Studies in Comparative Religion 2. Stockholm: Stockholm University.

Pedersen, Morten Axel. 2011. *Not Quite Shamans: Spirit Worlds and Political Lives in Northern Mongolia*. Cornell: Cornell University Press.

Peissel, Michael. 1984. *The Ants' Gold: The Discovery of the Greek El Dorado in the Himalayas*. London: Harvill.

Peters, Marion. 2008. *'Mercator Sapiens'*. Groningen: University of Groningen.

———— 2010. *De wijze koopman: het wereldwijde onderzoek van Nicolaes Witsen (1641–1717), burgemeester en VOC-bewindhebber van Amsterdam*. Amsterdam: Bakker.

Pfeiffer, Rudolf. 1957. 'Crusius, Otto'. In *Neue Deutsche Biographie 3*. Berlin: Duncker & Humblot, 432.

Pike, Kennet Lee. 1967. *Language in Relation to a Unified Theory of the Structure of Human Behavior*. 2nd ed. Mouton: The Hague.

—— 1990. *Emics and Etics: The Insider /Outsider Debate*. Th. N. Headland, *et al*. (eds.). Newbury Park: Sage Publications.

Pinker, Steven. 2011. *The Better Angels of Our Nature: Why Violence Has Declined*. New York: Viking.

Piras, Andrea. 2000. 'Le tre lance del giusto Wīrāz et la frescia di Abaris: Ordalia e volo estatico tra iranismo ed ellenismo'. In *Studi Orientali e Linguistici* 7:95–109.

—— 2014. Dialettiche dell'estasi. Sciamanesimo iranico e Zoroastrismo. In *Quaderni di Studi Indo-Mediterranei* 7, 155–181.

Protopopova, Nina I. [1999] 2003. *Éd'ii Dora*. Yakutsk: Bichik. [In Sakha, in Russian 2006].

Radloff, Wilhelm. 1884. *Aus Siberien: Lose Blätter aus dem Tagebuche eines reisenden Linguisten*. 2 vols. Leipzig: Weigel.

Reimann, Horst (ed.). 1984. *Bibliographie 1965–1984. Wilhelm Emil Mühlmann zum 80. Geburtstag*. Augsburg: Augsburg University.

Reimann, Horst & Kiefer, Klaus (eds.). 1964. *Bibliographie 1928–1964. Wilhelm Emil Mühlmann 60. Geburtstag*. Wiesbaden: Harassowitz.

Riboli, Diana & Torri, Davide (eds.). 2013. *Shamanism and Violence: Power, Repression and Suffering in Indigenous Religious Contexts*. Burlington: Ashgate.

Ricoeur, Paul. 2004. *Memory, History, Forgetting*. Translated by K. Blamey, D. Pellauer. Chicago: University of Chicago.

Robert, Luis. 1990. *Opera minora selecta* VII. Amsterdam: Hakkert.

Rohde, Erwin. 1894–1898. *Psyche*. 2 vols. Leipzig: Mohr.

Romanucci-Ross, Lola. 1977. 'The Hierarchy of Resort in Curative Practices: The Admiralty Islands'. In D. Landy (ed.). *Culture, disease and Curing*. New York: Macmillan, 481–87.

Romanova, Ekaterina N. 1994. *Yakutskii prazdnik ysyakh: istoki i predstavlenia*. Novosibirsk: Nauka.

—— 1997. *'Liudi Sol'nechnykh luchei s povod'iami za spinoi'. Sud'ba v kontekste miforitual'noi traditsii Yakutov*. Moscow: Russian Academy of Sciences.

———— 2008. 'Mifologiia sovremennogo shamanstva. K interpretatsii fenomena "pomniashaia kul'tura"'. In S. Iu. Nekliudov (ed.). *Mif, Simbol, Ritual. Narody Sibiri*. Moscow: RG Gumanitarnyie Universitet, 309–326.

Runeberg, Arne. 1947. *Witches, Demons and Fertility Magic. Analysis of their significance and mutual relations in West-European folk religion*. Societas Scientiarum Fennica. Commentationes Humanarum Litterarum XIV. 4. Helsingfors: SSF.

Russell, Donald Andrew. 1981. 'Eric Robertson Dodds'. In *Proceedings of the British Academy* 67:357–370.

Rzhevsky, Nicholas. 1996. *An anthology of Russian literature from earliest writings to modern fiction: introduction to a culture*. Armonk, New York: Sharpe.

Satta, Gino. 2005. 'Le fonti etnografiche de "Il mondo magico"'. In C. Gallini (ed.). *Ernesto de Martino e la formazione del suo pensiero. Note di metodo*. Napoli: Liguori, 57–77.

Scheltema, Jacobus. 1817–1819. *Rusland en de Nederlanden*. 4 vols. Amsterdam: Gartman.

Seymour, Henry Danbey. 1855. *Russia on the Black Sea and Sea of Azof: Being a Narrative of Travels in the Crimea and Bordering Provinces; with Notices of the Naval, Military, and Commercial Resources of Those Countries*. London: J. Murray.

Shirokogoroff, Sergei Michailovich. 1924. *Ethnical Unit and Milieu: A Summary of the Ethnos*. Shangai: E. Evans & Sons.

———— 1935. *The Psychomental Complex of the Tungus*. London: Kegan, Paul, Trench, Trubner.

———— 1999. *The Psychomental Complex of the Tungus*. Berlin: Reinhold Schletzler.

Snorri Sturluson. *Heimskringla: History of the Kings of Norway. Translated with Introduction and Notes by Lee M. Hollander*. Published for the American-Scandinavian Foundation by the University of Texas Press, Austin, 1964.

Snorri Sturluson. *Heimskringla I*. Íslenzk fornrit. XXVI. Bindi. Reykjavík 1979.

Strömbäck, Dag. 2000. *Sejd och andra studier i nordisk själsuppfattning*. Med bidrag av Bo Almqvist, Gertrud Gidlund, Hans Mebius. Redaktör Gertrud Gidlund. Acta Academiae Regiae Adolphi LXXII. Hedemora: Kungl. Gustav Adolfs Akademien för svensk folkkultur.

von Stuckrad, Kocku. 2003. *Schamanismus und Esoterik*. Leuven: Peeters.

———— 2012. 'Refutation and Desire: European Perceptions of Shamanism in the Late Eighteenth Century'. In *Journal of Religion in Europe* 5:100–121.

Taussig, Michael. 1987. *Shamanism, Colonialism and the Wild Man: A Study in Terror and Healing*. Chicago: University of Chicago Press.

Tavernier, Roger. 2006. *Russia and the Low Countries: An International Bibliography 1500–2000*. Groningen: Barkhuis.

Tedlock, Barbara. 2005. *The Woman in the Shaman's Body: Reclaiming the Feminine in Religion and Medicine*. New York: Bantam Dell.

———— 2008. 'Shamanism and Shamanic Practice Today and Into the Future'. In *Journal of Shamanic Practice* 1 (1):7–11.

Temir, Ahmet. 1955. 'Leben und Schaffen von Friedrich Wilhelm Radloff (1837–1918). Ein Beitrag zur Geschichte der Türkologie'. In *Oriens* 8:51–93.

Tiele, Pieter Anton. 1884, repr. 1966. *Nederlandsche bibliografie van land- en volkenkunde*. Amsterdam: Frederik Müller.

Tinker, George E. 2004. *Spirit and Resistance: Political Theology and American Indian Liberation*. Minneapolis: Fortress Press.

Thompson, Stith. 1961, 1987. *The Types of the Folktale. A Classification and Bibliography*. FF Communications. No. 184. Helsinki.

———— 1955–1958. *Motif-index of folk-literature : a classification of narrative elements in folktales, ballads, myths, fables, mediaeval romances, exempla, fabliaux, jest-books and local legends*. Copenhagen: Rosenkilde & Bagger.

Todd, Robert B. 1998. 'E.R. Dodds: a bibliography of his publications'. In Quaderni di Storia 48:175–194.

———— 1998. 'A Note on the Genesis of E.R. Dodds'. In *The Greeks and the Irrational*, Echos du Monde Classique / Classical Views 17:663–676.

———— 2004. 'Technique in the Service of Humanism: A.B. Poynton's Legacy to E.R. Dodds'. In *Eikasmos* 15:463–476.

———— 2005. '"His own side-show": E.R. Dodds and Neoplatonic Studies in Britain, 1835–1940', *Dionysius* 22:139–160.

———— 2005. 'E. R. Dodds: Bibliographical addenda'. In *Quaderni di storia* 61:221–224.

Tortorelli Ghidini, Marisa. 2015. Il volo dell'anima. Riflessioni sullo sciamanesimo Greco. In C. Giuffré Scibona and A. Mastrocinque (eds). *Studi in onore di Giulia Sfameni Gasparro*. Rome: Edizioni Quasar, 233–242.

Treichel, F. 1976. 'Ides'. In O. Klose & E. Rudolph (eds.). *Schleswig-Holsteinisches Biographisches Lexikon* IV. Neumünster: Wachholtz, 115–117.

Troshansky, V. F. 1903. *Evoliutsiia chernoi very (shamanstvo) u Yakutov*. Kazan: Uchenyi zapiski Kazanskogo universiteta.

Turner, Edith. 2006. *Among the healers: stories of spiritual and ritual healing around the world*. Westport and Conn.: Praeger Publishers.

Turner, Victor. 1972. 'Religious Specialists'. In D. L. Sills (ed.). *International Encyclopedia of the Social Sciences* 13. New York: Macmillan, 437–44.

———— 1977. 'Process, System and Symbol: A New Anthropological Synthesis'. In *Daedalus* 106 (3):61–80.

Vecsey, Christopher. 1981. *Introduction to Åke Hultkrantz. Belief and Worship in Native North America*. Edited, with an Introduction by Christopher Vecsey. Syracuse, New York: Syracuse University Press.

Vernant, Jean-Pierre. 1971. *Mythe et pensée chez les grecs*. 2 vols. Paris: Maspéro.

Vivieros de Castro, Eduardo. 1998. 'Cosmological Deixis and Amerindian Perspectivism'. In *The Journal of the Royal Anthropological Institute* 4 (3, Sept):469–488.

Wallace, Anthony F. C. 1956. 'Acculturation: Revitalization Movements'. In *American Anthropologist* 58 (2):264–281.

———— 1972. *Death and Rebirth of the Seneca*. New York: Vintage.

Weber, Max. [1922] 1963. *The Sociology of Religion*. Boston: Beacon.

Weiser, Lily. 1927. Altgermanische Jünglingsweihen und Männerbunde. Ein Bietrag zur deutschen und nordiscen Altertums- und Volkskunde. In *Bausteine zur Volkskunde und Religionswissenschaft. Herausgegeben von Eugen Fehrle*. Heft 1. Bühl (Baden): Konkordia.

West, Martin L. 2007. *Indo-European Poetry and Myth*. Oxford: Oxford University Press.

———— 2013. *Hellenica II*. Oxford: Oxford University Press.

West, Stephanie. 2004. 'Herodotus on Aristeas'. In C. Tuplin (ed.). *Pontus and the Outside World*. Leiden: Brill, 43–67.

Whitehead, Neil & Wright, Robin. 2004. *In Darkness and Secrecy: The Anthropology of Assault Sorcery and Witchcraft in Amazonia*. Durham: Duke University Press.

Willerslev, Rane. 2007. *Soul hunters: hunting, animism, and personhood among the Siberian Yukaghir*. Berkeley: University of California Press.

Wladimiroff, Igor. 2008. *De kaart van een verzwegen vriendschap. Nicolaes Witsen en Andrej Winius en de Nederlandse cartografie van Rusland*. Groningen: University of Groningen.

Wuthnow, Robert. 2007. *After the Baby-boomers*. Princeton: Princeton University Press.

Yakovlev, Viliam I. 2000. *Erkeeni khohotyn ytyk sidere [Sacred Places in the Erkeeni Valley]* Shadrina, G., sos. Sviashennye i pamiatnye mesta Khangalas. Yakutsk: IGI. [in Sakha].

Zhmud, Leonid. 2012. *Pythagoras and the Early Pythagoreans*. Oxford: Oxford University Press.

Znamenski, Andrei. 2003. *Shamanism in Siberia: Russian records of indigenous spirituality.* Dordrecht and Boston MA: Kluwer Academic Publishers.

———— 2007. *The Beauty of the Primitive: Shamanism and the Western Imagination.* New York: Oxford University Press.

Author Presentations

Jan N. Bremmer was born in 1944 in Groningen in the North of the Netherlands. He studied Classics and Spanish at the Free University, Amsterdam (1962–1970). From 1970–1972 he did his military service in the Dutch Military Intelligence. In 1979 he received his PhD from the Free University with his dissertation *The Early Greek Conception of the Soul*, which was published in 1983 by the Princeton University Press. His Greek Religion (1994) has been translated into Dutch, German, Italian, Spanish and French. In 1990, he was appointed to the Chair of Religious Studies at the Faculty of Theology and Religious Studies of the University of Groningen, where he was dean of the Faculty for nearly 10 years (1996–2005). He retired at the end of 2009.

Bremmer specialises in Greek, Roman, early Christian and contemporary religion and the historiography of ancient religion. His publications range from Greek and Roman Mythology and religion, the apocryphal traditions about Jesus' apostles, life after death, ancient humor and magic to modern secularisation and contemporary New Age. More recently, he was a Fellow of the Internationales Kolleg Morphomata (Cologne: 2010–2011), the Inaugural Gastprofessor für Kulturgeschichte des Altertums (Munich: 2011–2012), Visiting Research Scholar, Institute for the Study of the Ancient World (New York: 2012–2013), Fellow, Max-Weber-Kolleg (Erfurt: 2013–2014, 2016), Visiting Professor at the Sonderforschungsbereich 948 (Freiburg/Br: 2014) and Macquarie Ancient Cultures Research Centre Visiting Research Fellow (Sydney: 2016). In the spring of 2006 his contributions to scholarship and university life were nationally recognised when the Queen appointed him Officer in the Order of Orange–Nassau. ORCID ID: http://orcid.org/0000-0001-8400-7143

Ulf Drobin (1935-) began his academic career at Stockholm University in the early 1960s as a student of German and Nordic languages. A fascination for the intricacies of Old Icelandic poetry led him to pursue advanced studies in the history of religions at the Department of Comparative Religion, were he received his doctorate under the tutelage of Åke Huntkranz in 1983, and continued to serve as senior lecturer and adjunct professor until his retirement in 1999. Drobin has been especially interested in the theoretical foundations of the study of religion, including the interface between comparative religion and folklore, western perceptions of African religions, and the implicit assumptions behind the Indo-European so-called Stammbaum model.

Carlo Ginzburg was born in 1939. He has held positions at the University of Bologna, at UCLA, at the Scuola Normale di Superiore di Pisa. Among his numerous and strongly influential studies are *The Cheese and the Worms: The Cosmos of a Sixtenth Century Miller* (English translation 1980), *The Night Battles: Witchcraft and Agrarian Cults in the Sixteenth and Seventeenth Centuries* (English translation 1983), and *Ecstasies: Deciphering the Witches' Sabbath* (English translation 1991). ORCID ID: http://orcid.org/XXX

Peter Jackson is Professor of the History of Religions at Stockholm University. He specializes in the study of Indo-European religions, with particular emphases on Ancient India and Iran, Mediterranean antiquity, and the pagan Germanic world. Among his recent publications are the co-edited volumes *Philosophy and the End of Sacrifice: Disengaging Ritual in Ancient India, Greece, and Beyond* (Equinox, 2015) and *Transforming Warriors: The ritual organization of military force* (Routledge, 2016). ORCID ID: http://orcid.org/000-002-0742-6640

Marjorie Mandelstam Balzer, Research Professor in CERES and the Department of Anthropology at Georgetown University (Washington), and a Fellow at the American Museum of Natural History (New York). She has research interests in ecology, religion, inter-ethnic relations, the dynamics of nationalism, and the anthropology of the Russian Federation. She has done extensive fieldwork, focusing on Siberia and Central Asia, regularly traveling to the Far East (Sakha Republic), and working collaboratively with indigenous scholars in the U.S. and Siberia. A current book ms. compares political and cultural revitalization in three republics within the Russian

Federation, Sakha (Yakutia), Buryatia, and Tuva. She has taught at the University of Illinois and the University of Pennsylvania, and held post-doctoral fellowships at Harvard, Columbia, and the Woodrow Wilson Center. Author of The Tenacity of Ethnicity: A Siberian Saga in Global Perspective and Shamans, Spirituality and Cultural Revitalization, she has edited numerous collections including Shamanic Worlds: Rituals and Lore of Siberia and Central Asia. As editor of the journal Anthropology and Archeology of Eurasia, she helps scholars from the former Soviet Union be published in English. She is especially proud to have helped organize exchanges between Native Siberian and Native American leaders. ORCID ID: http://orcid.org/0000-0002-7048-996X

Index

www.ingramcontent.com/pod-product-compliance
Lightning Source LLC
Chambersburg PA
CBHW051435270326
41935CB00019B/1835